Other *Wesley Study Bible* Resources

Reading Scripture as Wesleyans by Joel B. Green

The Grace-Filled Life: 52 Devotions to Warm Your Heart and Guide Your Path by Maxie Dunnam

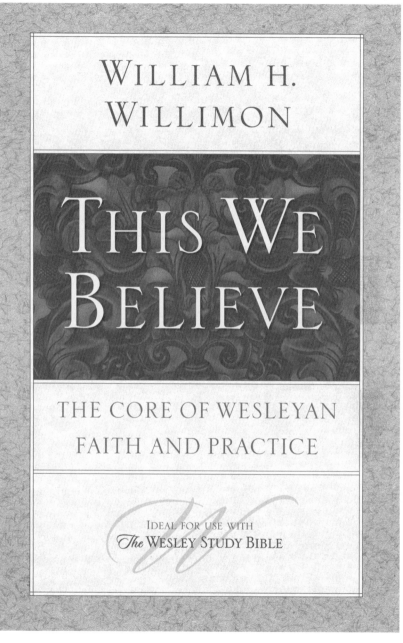

WILLIAM H. WILLIMON

THIS WE BELIEVE

THE CORE OF WESLEYAN FAITH AND PRACTICE

IDEAL FOR USE WITH
The WESLEY STUDY BIBLE

Abingdon Press
Nashville

THIS WE BELIEVE
THE CORE OF WESLEYAN FAITH AND PRACTICE

This book is printed on acid-free paper.

Library of Congress Cataloging-in-Publication Data

Willimon, William H.
   This we believe : the core of Wesleyan faith and practice / William H. Willimon.
     p.   cm.
   Includes index.
   ISBN 978-1-4267-0689-9
   1. Methodist Church—Doctrines.   2. Wesley, John, 1703–1791.   I. Title.
   BX8331.3.W55   2010
   230'.7—dc22

                                                                    2009036608

11 12 13 14 15 16 17 18 19—10 9 8 7 6 5 4

MANUFACTURED IN THE UNITED STATES OF AMERICA

To

Wesley Garrett at his baptism:

Welcome to the adventure of Wesleyan Christianity

CONTENTS

INTRODUCTION

I believe that . . ." "I have faith in . . ." What we believe is that which we trust, that which we know to be true. Critical reflection upon what we believe is that enterprise we call *theology*. Everybody does theology, even when we don't know that's what we're doing. Theology (literally, "talk about God") is what we do when something very bad happens to us (Why me?) or something quite wonderful happens to us (Why me?). The one whom you address in such moments, that Being beyond your being, is your God, even if you're not conscious of the one to whom you are speaking. Why am I here? What's the point of it all? Is this all there is? After death, what? Who is God? What does God want from me? Theology deals with these deep, dangerous questions that defy easy answers—which may be one reason why most people get nervous if ever their preacher should announce, "And now I'm going to do some theology."

More important, theology is what nearly everyone does when he or she is met by Jesus Christ. Theology in the sense of what Jesus Christ evokes in us is God's talk to us, that which the living God lovingly says to the world. Thus John's Gospel introduces Jesus as "the Word," God's great address to God's creation. Some people heard "the Word" as God's word spoken to them, and some didn't. Something about Jesus leads people to say things like, "Here is the long-awaited Savior of the world!" or "He can't be the Son of God, can he?" or "Where did you get all this stuff?" or "We never heard anything like this." From the first, it was nearly impossible to say anything about Jesus without raising a question like, "Who is God, anyway?"

I don't mean to say that everybody does *good* theology. Good, faithful, specifically Christian theology is theology that is informed by and responsive to Scripture, the historic faith of the church, and the promptings of the Holy Spirit right now in our lives. There is well-formed informed theology, and then there is theology that is merely "what seems right to me" or "here is the latest idea on Twitter."

In this book I will attempt to help you do the former using a valuable new resource—*The Wesley Study Bible* (*WSB*). Christians don't have to reinvent the wheel, theologically speaking. We have faithful guides who will show us the way if we will dare listen. Faithful Christian theology arises in conversation with the saints of the past (Scripture), who tell us what they discovered about God when God discovered them. The *WSB* is unique in making explicit how, when we read Scripture, we join a lively conversation of the living and the dead that began long before we got here and shall continue long after we are gone. Scripture is highly charged, visionary literature that stokes, funds, and fuels our imaginations, presenting us with a more interesting world than we would have had if we had been left to our own devices. All our theology is accountable to Scripture; the Bible keeps our thought focused on the God who, in Jesus Christ, has so graciously focused on us.

Do not attempt theology at home! You can't do faithful Christian theology on your own—thinking about God is a group activity. Our God is so wonderfully complex, dynamic, mysterious, and counter to whom we expect God to be that you need help from your friends to think about the Trinity. The Bible is the product of the church's life with God, and Scripture's primary audience is the church. As Wesley said, Christianity is a "social religion"—you can't do it alone.

The Wesley Study Bible can be read solo but is best read with a group of friends in your church. But even they are too limited a group of interlocutors. Fortunately, one of the great gifts of *The Wesley Study Bible* is its introduction to a host of new friends, chief among them the brothers John and Charles Wesley, friends living, and friends dead, including

Matthew, Mark, Luke, John, Mary, Sarah, Miriam, and all the rest of the Bible's witnesses who are eager to have a lively conversation with you about theology.

Although you may not have been thinking about God in Jesus Christ that long, don't worry: the brothers Wesley took as their special mission to introduce people to the living God. Their heirs in the Methodist movement have been talking about God to anybody who will listen for more than two hundred years. They have a lot to say.

The good news is that you don't have to come up with words about God—theology—on your own. Wesleyan Christians are those who think about God along with the Wesleys. The theological revolution begun in eighteenth-century England has now spread to every corner of the globe. Millions have met the true and living God through the ministrations of the Methodists, heirs of Wesley. *The Wesley Study Bible* is presented as an exchange among the diverse speakers within Scripture (those in Israel and the early church who had so vivid an encounter with God that they just had to talk about and figure out what had happened to them) and (in the sidebars in the *WSB*) a conversation between the Wesleys and Wesleyans on their particular experience of God. There are also the sidebar testimonies of present-day pastors on the life applications for the biblical and Wesleyan insights. "Warm hearts and active hands" is a good summary of theology in the Wesleyan tradition.

As your theological guide, I will refer frequently to the

Wesleyan Core Term sidebars by putting the page numbers from the relevant *WSB* sidebars in the text. You can read this book and do the theology without having the *WSB* in hand and without looking up the cited core terms, but I hope that you will make this a true theological conversation by reading with this book in one hand and the *WSB* in the other.

You don't have to be a Wesleyan to do faithful Christian theology, but forgive me for thinking that it really helps. John and Charles Wesley's discoveries about God still astound and challenge us today. The worldwide renewal of the church launched by the Wesleys has exceeded their wildest dreams. Wesleyan *practical divinity* (one of John Wesley's favorite terms for his sort of theology) is as revolutionary and as badly needed today as ever.

Mark said that while Jesus was hurrying down the road, a man stopped him and asked a deep theological question: "What must I do to inherit eternal life?" (Mark 10:17-31). One Gospel stated that the man was a "ruler"; another noted that he was "young." All agreed that he was "rich." At first Jesus brushed him off with, "You know what Scripture says—obey the Ten Commandments."

"I've obeyed all the commandments since I was a kid," replied the man. (Never broken a commandment? Who among us could say that? This man was not only successful in accumulating wealth; he was successful at morality too.)

Then Mark stated, "Jesus looked at him and loved him"—
the only time that Jesus is said to have loved a specific individual. Then, in one of the wildest demands Jesus ever
made of anybody (because "he loved him"?), Jesus told the
man to "go, sell all you have, give it to the poor, then come,
follow me."

With that, Mark said, the young man got depressed and
departed, leaving Jesus to lament, "It is very difficult to save
those who have lots of stuff."

While the North American in me is distinctly uneasy
about Jesus treating affluent people in this brusque way, the
Wesleyan in me loves Jesus' response to the man's big theological question. Refusing to be drawn into an intellectual
bull session, some ethereal blather about "eternal life"
(which Jesus discussed only rarely), Jesus hit the man not
with ideas about eternity but with ethics here on earth—the
Ten Commandments, redistribution of wealth, moral transformation, discipleship. Here this rather smug, successful
person attempted to lure Jesus into abstract, speculative
theology; and Jesus, after citing scripture, forced the man
to talk about obedience and action. Jesus didn't urge him
to "think," "ponder," or "reflect." Rather, he spoke to him
only in active verbs: "Go . . . sell . . . give . . . follow me."

To my mind, it was a wonderfully Wesleyan theological
moment (see *WSB* 1223). The man wanted a relaxed discussion; Jesus got practical and demanding. Jesus never said,
"Think about me!" He said, "Follow me!" All the man might

have wanted was a polite exchange of ideas about eternal life, but what he got was a call to go, sell, give, and be a disciple.

When Wesley discussed this passage in his *Explanatory Notes on the New Testament*, he focused on both Jesus' love for this person and the need for loving personal response to that love. Wesley praised "the love of God, without which all religion is a dead carcass." Then he exhorted readers, "In order to [obtain] this, throw away what is to thee the grand hindrance of it. Give up thy great idol, riches."

I think Mark 10:21-22 is the only place in the Gospels where someone is called by Jesus to be a disciple and refuses. Yet for all that, it's one of the most explicitly Wesleyan gospel moments. God's love is gracious but also demanding. Wesley was not much interested in any theology that couldn't be put into practice; warmed hearts and good intentions were no substitutes for active hands. And the point of having deep conversations with Jesus about what to believe was to be better equipped to obey Jesus. Theological reflection on Jesus was in service of better following Jesus. And even Jesus' demands upon us—his call for relinquishment and giving—were gracious testimony to his love for us. To think in this fashion is theology in the Wesleyan spirit. In his short tract "The Character of a Methodist" (available at http://new.gbgm-umc.org/umhistory/wesley/character/), Wesley noted that Methodism is distinguished not by unique doctrines but by a shared commitment to theological renewal and active obedience to a living Lord.

Wesley believed that theology was always in service to practical Christian living. Therefore, he urged that theology be done in the mode of "plain truth for plain people" (see *WSB* 592). I hope that this book will do just that for you. Two great contemporary United Methodist theologians aided me in writing this book: Richard Heitzenrater, who time and again has been my teacher in Wesley, and Randy Maddox, whose approach to Wesleyan theology in his classes at Duke has been indispensable in the composition of this book. Although they do not agree with everything I've said here, they gave most gracious (oh, what Wesleyans they are!) assistance to me in this project. Welcome to the adventure of talking about and thinking about God in a practical, grace-induced, Wesleyan way.

William H. Willimon

ABBREVIATIONS

BOD   *The Book of Discipline of The United Methodist Church*. Nashville: The United Methodist Publishing House, 2008.

HGEL   Charles Wesley. *Hymns on God's Everlasting Love; To Which Is Added the Cry of the Reprobate and the Horrible Decree*. Bristol: Farley, 1741. Accessed at www.divinity.duke.edu/wesleyan/texts/cw_published_verse.html.

HSP (1739)   John and Charles Wesley. *Hymns and Sacred Poems*. London: Strahan, 1739. Accessed at www.divinity.duke.edu/wesleyan/texts/jw_poetry_hymns.html.

HSP (1740)   John and Charles Wesley. *Hymns and Sacred Poems*. London: Strahan, 1740. Accessed at

www.divinity.duke.edu/wesleyan/texts/jw
_poetry_hymns.html.

Hymn (1780) John Wesley. *A Collection of Hymns for the People Called Methodists*. London: Paramore, 1780. Accessed at http://wesley.nnu.edu/charles_wesley/hymns/index.htm.

Notes John Wesley. *Explanatory Notes upon the New Testament*. New York: J. Soule and T. Mason, 1818.

UMH *The United Methodist Hymnal*. Nashville: The United Methodist Publishing House, 1989.

WSB Joel B. Green and William H. Willimon. *The Wesley Study Bible*. Nashville: Abingdon Press, 2009.

CHAPTER ONE

WE BELIEVE IN ONE GOD— FATHER, SON, AND HOLY SPIRIT

Amid the numerous and often acrimonious theological disputes of his day, John Wesley was unusually generous and charitable in his theology. "Keep close to the grand scriptural doctrines," he advised his Methodists, urging them to avoid unproductive, theological hairsplitting.

> There are many doctrines of a less essential nature, with regard to which even the sincere children of God (such is the present weakness of human understanding!) are and have been divided for many ages. In these we may think and let think; we may "agree to disagree." But, meantime, let us hold fast the essentials of "the faith which was once delivered to the saints," . . . insisted on at all times and in all places. (Sermon preached on the death of George Whitefield, 1770)

At our best, this has led us later-day Wesleyans to hold fast to the great tradition of biblical Christianity without being drawn into squabbles over nonessentials. At our worst, this generous Wesleyan "think and let think" has led to our acting as if ideas about God are not that important after all and to the sad error of thinking that because thought about God is inconsequential, who cares what anybody believes as long as that belief is sincerely held?

Wesley was a fierce foe of this sort of goofy theological "indifferentism." So is the Bible. Jesus Christ clearly caused a theological crisis. When people met him, they were forced to rethink their received and cherished ideas about God and themselves. To say that we don't know everything we might like to know about God does not excuse us from the responsibility to think on the basis of what has been revealed to us and to bet our lives on what we know.

To begin with the "faith which was once delivered unto the saints," let us begin with God. Christians believe that in the life, death, and resurrection of Jesus Christ, we have seen as much of God as we ever hope to see. As 1 John declares, "No one has ever seen God" (4:12). I daresay that most people, if they ever get around to thinking about God, think of God as whatever or whoever is large, distant, and invisible. God is unfathomable, beyond reach of our thinking and perceiving.

Christians admit that it may be of the nature of God to be beyond human visibility or comprehension. *Until Jesus Christ.* Jesus Christ is the full, perfect, sufficient revelation

WE BELIEVE IN ONE GOD

of who God is and what God does. Everything we believe about God flows from what we've seen of God in Jesus Christ. Although Wesley made allowances for everybody, even those who didn't know Christ, to have some implicit knowledge of God through the working of prevenient grace (more about that later), knowledge of God is necessarily imperfect until it is knowledge that is explicitly derived from encounter with Christ. Wesleyans believe that in Jesus Christ, God gets personal, relational, available, and virtually unavoidable.

In his first Advent among us, Jesus as the "Son of God," the "Messiah" (that is, "anointed one of God") challenged how people thought about God. Lots of people looked at Jesus, listened to his teaching, witnessed his work, saw his death, and said, "That's not God. God is powerful, distant, high, and lifted up. God is _____." (Fill in the blank with whatever high and noble attribute God simply must have if God is to be worthy of your worship.) Jesus failed to measure up to their preconceptions of who God ought to be and how God is to act if God is really God.

Especially today, to stand and affirm, with the Apostles' Creed—"I believe in God the Father Almighty . . . and in Jesus Christ, his only Son our Lord. . . . [And] I believe in the Holy Spirit"—is to assert a considerably more complex and challenging view of God than that which prevails among most Americans.

Most people in our society appear to want God to be generic, abstract, vague, distant, and arcane. "God? Oh, can't say anything too definite about God. God is large and indistinct." For many of us God is this big, blurry concept that we can make to mean about anything we like, something spiritual, someone (if we have any distinct notions about God) whom we can make over so that God looks strikingly like us.

In Jesus of Nazareth, God got physical, explicit, and peculiar, and God came close—too close for comfort for many. Jesus Christ is God in action, God refusing to remain a general idea or a high-sounding principle. Jesus Christ is God in motion toward us, God refusing to stay enclosed in God's own divinity. Many people think of God as a vaguely benevolent being—who never actually gets around to *doing* anything.

It is as if we are threatened by the possibility that God might truly be an active, intervening God who shows up where we live. We've designed this modern world, controlled by us, functioning rather nicely on its own, thank you, everything clicking along in accord with natural laws, served on command by technological wonders of our creation. So who needs a God who relishes actually showing up and doing something? We modern people are loath to conceive of a God who is beyond our control or a world other than the one that is here solely for our personal benefit.

This is the deistic God of the philosophers, a minimalist, inactive, unobtrusive, noninvasive, detached God who is just about as much of a God as we moderns can take. There's a reason why many thoughtful modern people seem so determined to sever Jesus from the Trinity, to render Jesus into a wonderful moral teacher who was a really nice person, someone who enjoyed lilies and was kind to children and people with disabilities. To point to a peripatetic Jew from Nazareth who wouldn't stay confined within our boundaries for God and say, "Jesus is not only a human being but also God," well, it's just too unnerving for us enlightened modern people to handle. Note how frequently many people refer to "God" and how seldom they refer to "Christ," and you will know why the statement "in Christ God was reconciling the world to himself" (2 Cor. 5:19) is a threatening disruption to many people's idea of a God who stays put.

John Wesley did not think of himself as a theological innovator, particularly in his thoughts about God. Wesley fully affirmed the traditional Articles of Religion of the Church of England, passing them on, with a few revisions, to the Methodists in North America (his "poor sheep in the wilderness") as the valid, biblical affirmation of faith. These revised articles are still printed toward the beginning of the United Methodist *Book of Discipline*. Here's Article 1 (with a line drawn through the portion removed by early Methodists):

There is but one living and true God, everlasting, without body or parts, ~~or passions,~~ of infinite power, wisdom, and goodness; the maker and preserver of all things, both visible and invisible. And in unity of this Godhead there are three persons, of one substance, power, and eternity—the Father, the Son, and the Holy Ghost.

All of this is fine, as far as it goes. But although he affirmed this article of religion, in actual practice Wesley emphasized something about God that led Wesley to distinctive thought about God. God was not only the "maker" of all reality but also the "preserver." On the basis of what he knew of God in Jesus Christ, Wesley stressed God as "Sovereign" and as an active, loving Parent. The person who knows Christ "knows God: his Father and his friend, the parent of all good, the centre of the spirits of all flesh, the sole happiness of all intelligent beings. He sees, clearer than the light of the noonday sun, that this is the end of man: to glorify him who made him for himself, and to love and enjoy him for ever" (Sermon 33, "Sermon on the Mount, XIII," §II.2).

> God's chief characteristic—even more than power, justice, or righteousness—is active, initiating, seeking love.

GOD OF LOVE

God's chief characteristic—even more than

power, justice, or righteousness—is active, initiating, seeking love. In his *Notes* on 1 John 4:8, "God is love," Wesley mused, "God is often styled holy, righteous, wise; but not holiness, righteousness, or wisdom in the abstract, as he is said to be love; intimating that this is his darling, his reigning attribute, the attribute that shed an amiable glory on all his other perfections."

In a sermon Wesley said that God "can do whatever he pleases. He can strike me or you dead in a moment" (and well we deserve it, I might add). But God doesn't because God "loves you; he loves to do you good. He loves to make you happy. Should not you then love *him*? And he will teach you how to love him" (Sermon 94, "On Family Religion," §III.7). Here most of Wesley's assertions about the nature of God are linked immediately to practical implications for us. God not only loves us but "loves to do [us] good," not only seeks our love but teaches us "how to love him." Our love of God is responsive, responsible love. Of 1 John 4:19, "We love because he first loved us," Wesley said in his *Notes*, "This is the sum of all religion." It wasn't so much that Wesley affirmed that God is love; any number of Christian traditions do the same. It was that Wesley relentlessly repeated that God's love evokes our love. God's love evokes, enables, and even requires our response. This Wesleyan interplay between theological assertion and practical human implication is the main reason *The Wesley Study Bible* is full of sidebars that offer practical, pastoral insights in response to Scripture's many grand theological affirmations.

Wesley's God is not simply full of love as an inclination or disposition. God is love in action. God did not sit on high serenely pronouncing, "I love you. Promise me you won't change a thing." God came to us as Jesus Christ, reaching toward us, transforming us with his touch. What is God like? God, taught Jesus, is like the woman who searches for one lost coin; the shepherd who relentlessly seeks the one lost sheep until he finds it; the father who eagerly awaits the return of the profligate son so he can welcome him not with harsh lectures and justly deserved paternal punishment but with an extravagant party (Luke 15).

This is a chief difference in the Wesleyan experience of God when compared with many current concepts of God. Wesley didn't just teach some banal platitude like "God is love"; he taught that God is wonderfully interactive, resourceful, responsive love, love that not only acts for us, in the cross and the Resurrection, on the vast stage of world history but also graciously acts in us, deep within our souls, activating our hands and feet in witness and service, so that we adoringly respond to the God who has so lovingly responded to us. "The life of God in the soul of a believer . . . immediately and necessarily implies the continual inspiration of God's Holy Spirit: . . . a continual action of God upon the soul, the re-action of the soul upon God" (Sermon 19, "The Great Privilege of those that are Born of God," §III.2).

An often repeated criticism of Jesus was that he "welcomes sinners and eats with them" (Luke 15:2). Jesus constantly intruded where he was not invited, sometimes where he was not wanted. The

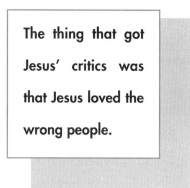

The thing that got Jesus' critics was that Jesus loved the wrong people.

thing that got Jesus' critics (at least those in Luke 15) was not that Jesus loved people but that Jesus received, ate with, and thereby loved the wrong people. Thus Jesus showed us not only that God is love but also that God's love was considerably more interesting, active, expansive, and determined than most of what passes for "love" around here (see *WSB* 180). In Jesus Christ, God was not only loving us but was also God *with* us, Emmanuel. As Charles Wesley said of the active Christ in one of his greatest hymns:

> He left his Father's throne above
> (so free, so infinite his grace!),
> emptied himself of all but love,
> and bled for Adam's helpless race. (*UMH*, 363)

THESE THREE ARE ONE

Wesleyans have historically practiced a robust trinitarianism. With all orthodox Christians at all times and places we have maintained that God is one; but not simply one, not merely one. We baptize in the name of the Trinity (see *WSB* 1165), thus signifying that baptism relates us to the fullness of God. We are monotheists (believers in one God) but not mere monotheists. We believe that the God who is present to us as Father, Son, and Holy Spirit is one. Father, Son, and Holy Spirit are three distinct yet unified and interactive, relational, and loving ways in which God is one. The Trinity is God in three ways being the same God.

If all this talk of three-in-one seems a bit overwhelming to you, you are not alone. Unitarianism is always a bit easier on the brain than trinitarianism. Still, there is no way for us to do justice to the God whom we have met in Jesus Christ without believing three ways in one God. Perhaps the Trinity is best approached not in analysis but in poetry, as in this Charles Wesley hymn, "Communion of Saints":

> Father, Son, and Spirit, hear
> Faith's effectual, fervent prayer,
> Hear, and our petitions seal;
> Let us now the answer feel,
> Mystically one with thee,
> Transcript of the Trinity,
> Thee let all our nature own
> One in Three, and Three in One. (*HSP* [1740], 188)

To say with the Hebrew Scriptures, "Hear, O Israel: The LORD is our God, the LORD alone" (Deut. 6:4-9, see *WSB*

224), is to say not simply that there is just one God but also that the God of Israel is singular, the one and only God, the true God, whereas lots of our idolatrous god-substitutes are not (see *WSB* 16).

Here again, in my experience, the Wesleyan view of God challenges many modern folk. In order to keep God distant and vague (and *irrelevant*) many people want to keep God simple, uncomplicated, and abstract. These are the dear folk who say, "Well, I'm not sure that I'm very religious, but I do believe in God. After all, isn't that what it's all about?"

The problem is that once we discovered that God was in Christ, things got complicated not because the church wanted to make the simple faith of Jesus complex and confusing but because we discovered in Jesus that God was at once much more demanding and much more interesting than we had first thought. In Christ, God was reiterated in ways that meant we were forced to expand our notions of God. We could have gotten along quite nicely without the Trinity had John the Baptist not intruded into our settled arrangements with God by shouting, "Here is the Lamb of God who takes away the sin of the world!" (John 1:29). Once Jesus showed up—one "conceived by the Holy Spirit," born of a poor peasant woman in Judea, God in the flesh, teaching, working wonders among us in the "power of the Spirit," suffering and dying at our hands, rising after three days, returning to the very people who crucified him, breathing his Holy Spirit upon us—well, we had to talk about God in a way that only complex, dynamic trinitarian theology could do justice. After being met by Jesus, we could never again think of God in the simple, uncomplicated way as we had before.

1. *God is the creative, caring Father,* but not simply at the beginning of creation. John Wesley believed that the same darkness-to-light, nothing-worked-up-into-something of Genesis 1 continues every day of our lives. God keeps creating, bringing something out of nothing, making a way when there was thought to be no way. God keeps caring, keeps reaching out to us in active love, constantly watches over us in vigorous providential care (see *WSB* 58).

Most of us, if we think about it, tend to think of God's providence in a rather general, abstract way—God cares but in an overall, cosmic way of caring. God got the world started, then left. Wesley taught a much more immediate, every-step-of-life's-way sort of providential care in which we are surprised to discover, often in the backward glance, that God has been lovingly leading us along, even when we didn't know God was leading us (see *WSB* 25, 605, 929). Seemingly small, unimportant events take on deeper significance when framed as possible moments of divine interaction with us.

But we must do nothing, in thinking about God's providential care, that limits or confines God. For instance, it is fashionable for some today to speak of God's having a "plan for my life" or God's "always being in control." I think this is what's left of the traditional doctrine of the providence of

God, the residue of the classical notion of the sovereignty of God. To my mind, talk of this sort risks making God's providence into rigid fate or destiny, which Wesley would have been loath to do. It risks reducing the sweeping cosmic, eternal work of God to a rather trivial step-by-step plan for my life.

Providence, at least for Wesley, means that although God could be in control of the world or have some prescribed, micromanaged plan for each of our lives, God chooses instead to love us. God conceivably could have made us into mindless robots, hardwired to do only what God wills, but instead God created us as those who are graciously invited to work with God in accomplishing God's good purposes for the world, a cooperation that is considerably more honorific than mere control. True freedom to say yes to God entails a counterfreedom to stupidly say no. It wouldn't be love for God if we had no real ability to turn away from or turn toward God. God makes promises to preserve us and always to love us, and God faithfully keeps those promises in a more dynamic manner than following a mere plan. To reiterate, all we really know for sure about God is that which is revealed in Jesus Christ. Does what you know of Jesus, in his interaction with his disciples, suggest that his main concern is control?

2. *God is the redeeming, loving, seeking Son* who ventures forth like some prodigal son (Luke 15) to search out and to save lost humanity in the "far country" where we live.

When God decisively, revealingly came to us, God came to us as one of us. God got incarnate as a Jew from Nazareth who was born in a most embarrassing way to a young peasant woman, grew up to be a man about whom we know next to nothing save his three years as a young adult in ministry, and was tortured to death by the government. That one is God among us.

The Gospels don't tell us everything that Jesus said and did. They appear to limit themselves to only those words and events that are related to our redemption. The Gospels tell us only those things about Jesus that directly relate to God's doing something about the problem between God and us. The name Jesus (or Joshua) means "God saves," and the Gospels depict Jesus as God's answer to what's wrong between us and God, God's saving the world, "for God so loved the world" (John 3:16).

John Wesley exuberantly believed the orthodox view of God that is found in the Articles of Religion. But at a rather dull church meeting on Aldersgate Street, John Wesley experienced God's reaching toward him in a particularly vivid, vivifying, heartwarming way. The God of the Bible and the church became the God for *him*. In Wesley's account of that heartwarming experience he underlined that Christ "had taken away *my* sins, even *mine*" (see *WSB* 1289).

It is one thing to have a belief in God; it is quite another thing to have a personal experience of the living, seeking

God. It is one thing to believe that God is there; it is quite another matter to believe that God is there *for you*. It's fine to believe that God in Christ reconciles the world to himself; it's quite another thing to believe that God has stepped in and actually reconciled you. Methodism's historic stress on doctrine lived, experienced, and put into practice surely is indebted to Wesley's story. If a priggish little former Oxford don, a failed missionary, and someone who was pious to the point of being annoying could be encountered by God at a church meeting on Aldersgate Street, well, that suggests that God could get through to *anybody*. Even you.

As the writer to the church at Ephesus put it, "You who once were far off have been brought near by the blood of Christ. . . . [He] has broken down the dividing wall . . . between us" (Eph. 2:13-14). Here is a living, active, loving God who makes union and breaks barriers. When the far-off one who has been brought near is *you*, when the wall that has been kicked down is the wall that you built in a vain attempt to keep God out of *your* life, then you are well on your way to believing in the same God as the God of John and Charles Wesley (see *WSB* 605).

Much of the theology that I hear in our church (and, alas, much that I preach!) tends to stress the first person of the Trinity—God the creative, ordering, providential Father—rather than God the redeeming Son or God the relentlessly reaching Holy Spirit. The more chaotic and confusing our world becomes, it seems the more we need to stress God the Creator. ("God has a plan for your life!") However, Wesley, perhaps because of his experience of the active, reaching, seeking, redeeming Son, offers us an equally robust Christology, a vital stress on the second person of the Trinity—a lively view of Christ as Savior of the world. Today when many speak of the sovereignty of God, they seem usually to speak of God the Creator of the world. Wesley conceived of sovereignty not only in God's creation of the world but also in God's redemption of all people and all things to God (see *WSB* 1056).

Our story with God begins, in the Bible, with two new human beings, fresh, vulnerable, at home and at peace in a lush garden. In just a couple of chapters things quickly go bad as humanity rebels against God's good intentions for us and disobeys God's minimal demands ("Stay off that tree" [Gen. 2:17]), and the first child becomes the first murderer, bashing in the head of his own brother (Gen. 4:1-12). Alienation from God is the result of our lust to be gods unto ourselves (see *WSB* 11). Listen to the local or world news on any given day and you will hear what fresh outrage we have perpetrated, the latest proof that we have a serious neighbor problem and an even more serious God problem. What righteous, holy God would have anything to do with humanity—the embarrassingly inept, supposed summit of God's creation—the defaced image of God?

Our sin and rebellion make all the more remarkable the Bible's illustration of God's refusal to give up on us. God kept returning to us, in constant loving guidance, in the words of the Law, the testimony of the prophets, the apocalyptic visions of a better future, finally coming to us as God's own Son. Because we couldn't come to God, because we demonstrated time and again that we were powerless to do something about our God problem, God came to us and solved our God gap as only God could.

Atonement (at-one-ment) is the array of images and doctrines whereby we testify that God in Christ does something about our God problem (see *WSB* 142). Throughout the Old Testament, God continually returns to God's people, Israel, resumes the divine-human conversation, and redeems what we messed up. The biblical God is not only righteous and holy, but also relentlessly redemptive (see *WSB* 331). The biblical God tells us the truth about all the ways we have fallen "short of the glory of God" (Rom. 3:23) and unilaterally acts to draw us back into the sphere of God's glory. In Jesus' birth God comes to us, incarnate, in the flesh, in order to restore us to the creatures whom God created us to be. Charles Wesley put this poetically in his "Hymn for Christmas-Day" (compare "Hark! the Herald Angels Sing"):

1. Hark how all the welkin rings
   "Glory to the King of kings."
5. Light and life to all he brings,
   Ris'n with healing in his wings.
8. Now display thy saving pow'r,

Ruin'd nature now restore,

Now in mystic union join

Thine to ours, and ours to thine.

9. Adam's likeness, Lord, efface,

Stamp thy image in its place. (*HSP* [1739], 206–8)

I love that *The Wesley Study Bible* discusses free grace (see *WSB* 112) deep in the Old Testament, at Exodus 34, where God (once again) returned to us even after we had messed up and disobeyed the law and destroyed the tablets that God gave Moses on the mountain. God told Moses to cut a set of replacement tablets. Will God ever give up on this ragtag gang of infidels, rebels, and losers?

Apparently not. Why? Because the Lord is

a God merciful and gracious,

slow to anger,

and abounding in steadfast love and faithfulness.

(Exod. 34:6)

The same Father who created the world, the God who kept returning to Israel in mercy and graciousness, is one with the Son who came to us, sought us, and died for us.

As Charles sang it, "Amazing love! How can it be / That thou, my God, shouldst die for me?" (*UMH*, 363).

3. *God is the present, dynamic Holy Spirit* who is God near to us, God empowering us to do those things that we could never do on our own, God constantly revealing God to us, God talking to us about God. There are things that God

wants us to know, things that we cannot know except as revelation—as a gift of God working through the Holy Spirit. And there are things that God wants us to do that we cannot do except through the empowerment of God's Holy Spirit. As the fourth Article of Religion puts it: "The Holy Ghost, proceeding from the Father and the Son, is of one substance, majesty, and glory with the Father and the Son, very and eternal God."

The article affirms the relatedness of the Trinity. The Holy Spirit is not an exotic third kind of God or some strange phenomenon that is somewhat similar to God. "We believe in the Holy Spirit who proceeds from and is one in being with the Father and the Son." The Holy Spirit is more than some impersonal force, psychic energy, or indistinct power. The Holy Spirit has a personality because it is the spirit of the Father and of the Son, God in action, the God who not only loves, not only redeems, but now, presently, all the time, "convinces the world of sin," leads us "through faithful response to the gospel into the fellowship of the Church," and "comforts, sustains and empowers the faithful and guides them into all truth" (Article 3, Confession of Faith). In other words, the Holy Spirit is God in action, God revealed, God present. If there is one thing that distinguishes a Wesleyan view of God from the views of other Christians, it is our pneumatology (*pneuma*= "wind" or "spirit"), our exceedingly active, personal, relational doctrine of the Holy Spirit.

Many Pentecostal churches have their roots in Wesleyanism. Much of Methodism's evangelistic impulse, the tendency of Methodism to reach out into constantly expanding areas of human need and to embrace a wide array of doctrinal perspectives, as well as the tendency of Methodists to think of ourselves as a dynamic movement as much as an established church, all relate to Wesleyan pneumatology.

In a famous letter that he wrote to a Roman Catholic, in which he affirmed the commonality of many of their beliefs and his take on the orthodox Christian faith, Wesley confessed belief not only in

> the infinite and eternal Spirit of God, equal with the Father and the Son, to be not only perfectly holy in Himself, but [and here is the typically Wesleyan twist] the immediate cause of all holiness in us; enlightening our understandings, rectifying our wills and affections, renewing our natures, uniting our persons to Christ, assuring us of the adoption of sons, leading us in our actions, purifying and sanctifying our souls and bodies, to a full and eternal enjoyment of God. (Letter to a Roman Catholic, July 18, 1749, §8)

In this passage Wesley knew the Holy Spirit chiefly by the effects in us of the Spirit as the "cause of all holiness in us; enlightening our understandings, rectifying our wills and affections, renewing our natures, uniting . . . assuring . . . leading . . . purifying and sanctifying" us to "full and eternal enjoyment of God." In God the Son we have God's atoning and reconciling work for us. In God the Holy Spirit we have God's sanctifying and redeeming work in us, now, here.

Talk of this sort drove orthodox Lutherans and many of the Reformed through the roof. How dare Wesley claim that this much good is being done in us by the Holy Spirit? Convinced of the persistent, ineradicable quality of our sin, these Protestants felt that Wesley had a too extravagant view of what the Holy Spirit could do to transform our lives. We're sinners, said the Lutherans, and though we may be redeemed by Jesus on the cross, we never get over our sinfulness. We may have some momentary victories over sin, said the Calvinists, but these tend to be short-lived and we never get over our sinfulness. Wesley differed not because of his rosy view of human nature (Wesley asserted human depravity with the best of them), but because of his huge faith in the power of the Holy Spirit.

Christian theology has historically spoken of the missions (*missio*= "to send") of the Trinity, the way that God the Father sends God the Son into the world, the way that God the Father and the Son continually send the Holy Spirit into the world to continue God's creation and redemption of the world, and the way that the Holy Spirit was upon Jesus to preach deliverance to the captives (Luke 4). Thus Methodists, so impressed by the active work of the Holy Spirit, have traditionally practiced a "sent" ministry. Our pastors are not called by individual congregations but rather sent out, appointed to congregations where it has been deemed that they are most needed. A God who is constantly out making moves on the world produces a church and a ministry who are sent. (And you thought the itinerant system of sending and appointing clergy was simply the creation of authoritarian bishops!)

We shall have to think more about the Wesleyan experience of God in the next chapters. For now, let us simply note that Methodists relish our knowledge of God that comes through our experience of the work of God in our world and in our lives. We believe in the Trinity because we have been encountered by the Trinity, transformed by a power greater than ourselves, loved by a love greater than our love. This experience of encounter, transformation, and love suggests to us that God is more complicated and rich than we were first led to believe. In the sidebar discussion of grace (see *WSB* 1110), *The Wesley Study Bible* defines this key Wesleyan term in a dynamically trinitarian way by saying that "grace" is "grounded in the love and mercy of God the Father; especially manifest in the life, death, and resurrection of God the Son; and experienced through the work of God the Holy Spirit in our lives."

That's saying a mindful.

CHAPTER TWO

WE BELIEVE IN JESUS CHRIST AND HIS REIGN

I t's a story so strange we could not have dreamed it up by ourselves, this story of how God was incarnate in Jesus the Christ. An embarrassing pregnancy, a poor peasant couple forced to become refugees in Egypt soon after the birth of their baby, King Herod's slaughter of the Jewish baby boys in a vain attempt to put an end to this new King. From the beginning the story of Jesus is the strangest story of all. A Messiah who avoids the powerful and the prestigious and goes to the poor and the dispossessed? A Savior who is rejected by many of those whom he sought to save? A King who reigns from a bloody cross? Can this one with us be God?

And yet Christians believe that this story, for all its strangeness, is true. Here we have a truthful account of how our God read us back into the story of God. This is a truthful depiction not only of who God really is but also of how we who were lost got found, redeemed, restored, and saved by a God who refused to let our rejection and rebellion (our notorious God problem) be the final word in the story.

Jesus the Christ (*Christ* means "Messiah," "the Anointed One") was a human being, a man who was born in a human family, attended parties (he was accused of being a glutton and a drunkard by his critics), moved constantly around the area of Galilee, ran afoul of the governmental and religious authorities, taught through short, pithy stories (parables), did a number of surprising and utterly inexplicable "signs and wonders," and eventually was tortured to death in a horribly cruel form of punishment that the Romans used against troublesome Jews and rebellious troublemakers. A few days later Jesus' astonished followers proclaimed to the world that Jesus had been raised from the dead and had returned to them, commissioning them to continue his work. (This aspect of the story has always been somewhat of a reach for those who prefer their gods to be aloof, ethereal, and at some distance from the grubby particularities of this world.)

Although these are roughly the historical facts of Jesus from Nazareth, as is so often the case, the raw facts don't tell the whole story. From the first, many knew that Jesus was not only a perceptive, challenging teacher (*rabbi*, teacher, was a favorite designation for Jesus) but was also uniquely present God (*Emmanuel* means "God with us"). In a very short time Paul (whose letters are the earliest writings in the New Testament) could acclaim crucified and resurrected Jesus as the long-awaited Messiah, the Christ, the one who was the full revelation of God. Jesus was not only a loving and wise teacher; Jesus was God Almighty doing something decisive about the problems between us creatures and the Creator.

THE REDEEMER

Through the years, the church has struggled to describe the mystery of our redemption, our at-one-ment with God (see *WSB* 331). From the first, a gathering band of believers knew that somehow, in the life and death of Jesus, God had taken the horrible instrument of humiliation and death— the cross—and had thereby done something decisive about us and our sin. The historic problem between God and us had been solved (see *WSB* 1374).

A number of images have been used through the ages to help the church talk about this grand mystery of how God the Son worked our redemption. First, some interpreters proclaimed Jesus as a *ransom* for our sin. We who were held hostage by our sin were set free, liberated by the saving, costly action on the cross: "The Son of Man came not to be served but to serve, and to give his life a ransom for many" (Mark 10:45; compare Rom. 6:20-23). Irenaeus, the church's first great postbiblical theologian (first century C.E.), extensively developed the ransom view.

Second, in the early twelfth century, Anselm of Canterbury (ca. 1033–April 21, 1109) wrote a variation on the ransom view, the *substitutionary atonement*. Using the medieval feudal system of his time, in which vassals were beholden to their lords, Anselm said that we humans owe everything to God. When we sin, we fail to give God what we justly owe our Creator. God can't simply overlook our rebellion and debt; to do so would make God unjust, which God can't be and still be God. We have run up such enormous debts with God that we'll never be able to pay up. In a great act of mercy, Christ pays in our behalf what we, in our sin, can never repay. God provides the only sufficient payment for our sin—God's own good Son, who suffers and dies the death we deserved.

Third, although this substitutionary atonement had great favor in the church, within a century Peter Abelard (1079–1142) raised a series of objections to Anselm's formulation: What does it say about God to say that God demands the blood of an innocent like Jesus to pay up in order to reconcile the world? Abelard offered an alternative account of the redemptive work of Christ. In the life and death of Christ, we are given an example of love and sacrifice that transforms us by inspiring us to love God and neighbor in the way that we should have done all along. Christ's death is not so much a substitute for our justly deserved penalty or a ransom for our indebtedness but rather, by his suffering, is an empowering *moral influence* upon us. One problem with the moral influence metaphor is that down through the ages the church has been hard-pressed to cite concrete instances of how Christ's example has been a powerful motivation for our good behavior!

Abelard's moral influence theory tended to glorify suffering as redemptive in much the same way as Anselm's substitutionary atonement. It rather dangerously moved from Christ's full, perfect, sufficient sacrifice to say that we also ought to be making continuing sacrifices. The blood that Christ sheds, and the blood that the followers of Jesus are sometimes asked to shed in following Jesus, tended to be the blood payment that a righteous God demanded.

This blood sacrifice motif, while exalting the suffering of the saints down through the ages, also tended to be perverted into a glorification of our suffering as redemptive. Too many battered women have been told by the church, "Stick with your abusive husband because your suffering mirrors the suffering of Christ." Or else blood sacrifice has been exalted as the divinely ordained path to good. I heard a speaker at a Memorial Day commemoration say, "The blood shed by our soldiers is the cost we sometimes have to pay for our freedom." Sentiments like these have led many Christians to question the ultimate helpfulness of substitutionary and moral influence theories of the Atonement. There is a constant need, in speaking of the sacrifice that divine righteousness demands, to reiterate that Christ is the final sacrifice, a gift that only God can give and receive, thus ending for all time the need for our attempts at blood sacrifice.

Fourth, Paul sometimes spoke of Christ as a Victorious Conqueror who faces down the powers and principalities, enters enemy territory, and triumphs (Col. 2:15). Martin Luther enjoyed using this view of *Christ as Victor*. Christ didn't just inspire us to live better lives; he accomplished our liberation from the power of sin and death. Christ is the hero who went head-to-head with Satan and death and, not only on the cross but also in resurrection, won. While the Victorious Conqueror image is a vivid, mythical metaphor, some may question whether Jesus, the Prince of Peace, ought to be depicted as a strong warrior, even in metaphorical, spiritual battle with Satan. With all of its metaphorical baggage, is this an image that has much traction among modern people? There's still too much sin and heartache in the world for many to think that Christ's victory is undisputed or that his triumph over evil is accomplished.

Fifth, Athanasius (293–May 2, 373) depicted Jesus as Vicarious Healer (2 Cor. 5:15-21; Rom. 8:1-4) in which Christ cures what is wrong with us (*salve*, Latin, "to save," can also mean "to heal"). On the cross Christ worked *healing* for our sin sickness and, through the Holy Spirit, continues to render *therapy* whereby we are changed into beings closer to what God intended in creating us in the first place. Paul said that while the "creation waits with eager longing for the revealing of the children of God," caught in "sufferings" and "futility," the work that Christ began in the cross and the Resurrection will one day be fully accomplished as the "creation itself will be set free from its bondage to decay" (Rom. 8:18-21).

Wesley believed that our redemption, though accomplished, is even now being worked out in those who are being redeemed, even us. By the grace of God, we have been awakened to the fact of our redemption in Jesus Christ, and we are empowered to live different lives through the working of the Holy Spirit in us (see *WSB* 1377). God applies to us the therapy we need to recover from our sick descent into sin. On the cross Christ did not just work *for* us, but in our daily walk with Christ we are delighted to find that Christ works in us. We are changed.

Because you are attempting to do Wesleyan theology with the Bible in one hand and this book in the other, you will note that while all of these theories of the Atonement can claim some biblical justification, none of them are found, in fully wrought form, in Scripture. All theories of the Atonement are second-order theological reflection— thought in which the church engages after reading the scriptural narratives of Jesus' work among us. We are not forced to settle on one account of the Atonement; all are helpful in one way or another in characterizing the great mystery that occurred in the cross of Christ; all fall short, in different ways, of the full glory of what Christ did on our behalf.

> **Christ's sacrifice was a gift, an act of worship whereby we are purified and made ready to serve God.**

I think it significant that Wesley's expansive theology embraces, in one place or another, all of these ways of speaking of Christ's atoning work. At the same time Wesley seems to have simply affirmed the historic emphasis on Jesus' death as the remedy for our guilt, the shame of our sin, the defacement of God's original intentions for us, and our resulting alienation from God (see *WSB* 1374). Theories of the Atonement are metaphors that reveal and point to the wonder of what God has done for us in the cross and resurrection of Christ.

Wesley frequently spoke of Christ's sacrifice on the cross, seemingly to affirm the classical, substitutionary formulation. However, Wesley took a step that (while more typical of the Orthodox and Roman Catholics) few Protestants had been willing to take. Wesley was keen to stress that God's grace works in us not only to convince us that the problem between us and God, due to our sin, has been solved by God in Christ, but also to restore our capacity to love God and neighbor. Wesley's emphasis seems to be not so much on the Atonement as a bloody propitiation for our sin, a substitutionary, vicarious sacrifice that was made on behalf

of our indebtedness to a righteous God (although in his sermons Wesley frequently stressed the horror of Christ's suffering on the cross). Rather, Christ's sacrifice was more of a
gift, an act of worship whereby we are purified and made
ready to serve God in all that we do. Christ is a sacrifice of
purification (Rom. 3:24-26) that, just as fire purifies, ren-
ders even us purified and ready to stand before God in joyful service (see *WSB* 1373).

Wesley faithfully adopted the view of Anselm and many
others that Christ's work on the cross is God's gracious gift
to satisfy our offense against God's justice (Rom. 5:9-10).
But that did not stop Wesley from joining with Abelard in
seeing the cross as a dramatic, objective, inspiring display of
the lengths to which God's wondrous love would go to res-
cue us (Rom. 5:6-8), a model that we Christians, in grati-
tude for what Christ has done, can and should emulate in
our responsive love for God.

Wesley also developed the therapeutic emphasis of
Athanasius, believing that our justification really does lead
to transformation in our lives as we are drawn ever more
closely to God (see *WSB* 1211). That emphasis was one that
heirs of Calvin and Luther, so convinced of the invincibility
and the enduring quality of human sin, found exasperating
and objectionable in Wesley. Some have said that Wesley
practiced a *conjunctive theology* in which the little conjunction *and* plays an important role in holding otherwise different thoughts together in creative tension with one

another. Thus with some justification, we can speak of
Wesley as affirming the substitutionary and the moral influence theories of the Atonement *and* the healing, therapeutic view as well.

Both John and Charles Wesley wove the various atonement metaphors into their hymns and sermons. Here is a
great mystery of God at work in even the worst of human
sin (the cross) that is best pondered in poetry rather than
prose. In one stanza Charles spoke of Christ's work as
doing something about our guilt, reconciling us, pardoning
us, calling us, adopting us, and empowering us:

> 1. Arise, my soul, arise,
>   Shake off thy guilty fears.
> 5. My God is reconciled,
>   His pardoning voice I hear;
>   He owns me for his child,
>   I can no longer fear:
>   With confidence I now draw nigh,
>   And, Father, Abba, Father, cry!
>
> ("Arise, My Soul, Arise," *Hymn* [1780], 194)

On many Good Friday services, after I have attempted to
preach about the cross, my feeble atonement sermon has
been bested by the congregation's singing of "O Love
Divine" that sings more than I as a preacher could ever say:

> 1. O Love divine, what hast thou done!
>   The immortal God hath died for me!

> The Father's co-eternal Son
> Bore all my sins upon the tree.
> Th'immortal God for me hath died:
> My Lord, my Love, is crucified!
> 2. Is crucified for me and you,
> To bring us rebels back to God. (*UMH*, 287)

How can it be that God is not only holy, righteous, and demanding but also determinedly loving, not only loving humanity in general but also loving a lying, self-deceitful, pretentious sinner like me? It is a mystery, a wonder that is best believed by retaining it only as a wonderful mystery and an adorable wonder.

> 1. And can it be that I should gain
> An interest in the Savior's blood!
> Died he for me? who caused his pain!
> For me? who him to death pursued?
> Amazing love! How can it be
> That thou, my God, shouldst die for me?
> 5. No condemnation now I dread;
> Jesus, and all in him, is mine;
> Alive in him, my living Head,
> And clothed in righteousness divine,
> Bold I approach th'eternal throne,
> And claim the crown, through Christ my own. (*UMH*, 363)

It has been said that the best of Wesleyan theology is in our hymnbook. We Wesleyans sing ourselves into the faith, put it in poetry before we affirm it in creed. There is some truth, often the deepest, most sacred truth, that can be apprehended only metaphorically, poetically, in corporate song. Perhaps Scripture meant for its rich metaphors of the atonement of Christ to stay metaphors and not be reduced to doctrinal exposition? There was something about the Incarnation that caused the whole creation to burst into song, to resort to poetry in order to sing and to say the significance of the advent of Jesus Christ (note the many songs in the first chapters of Luke's Gospel).

The Bible seems to want to stimulate and to cultivate our imagination rather than to restrain it. Most scripture is highly metaphorical, nearly all in narrative, reluctant to define and explicate. In thinking about the Atonement let us determine to stay close to the actual, specific narratives of "God with us" that is scripture. We shall want to focus on the cross, yes, but we will also want to recall the nativity, the Incarnation, the teachings of Jesus, noting the company he kept at table with him, the way he was in prayer, his miraculous signs and wonders too. Much mischief has been done, in the history of Christian doctrine, in attempting to dryly define our doctrine rather than warmly sing our faith.

CHRIST IN ALL HIS OFFICES

"What a friend we have in Jesus, all our sins and griefs to bear," we love to sing. Jesus is that, but in Scripture, and in our own Wesleyan experience, he is even more.

Sometimes the greatest challenge of belief in Jesus Christ is to believe that Jesus is not only Friend, Lord, and Savior, but also Priest, King, and Sacrifice. The church has historically spoken of the *offices* of Christ. In Jesus Christ, God appeared to us and was active for us in a rich array of works. To say "Jesus Christ is Lord" is to say something about who Christ is and about what Christ did and what Christ does.

In every age church history shows that the people of God have a tendency to reduce the work of Christ to whatever office is most congenial to the age. The Wesleys emphasized a rich, balanced view of Christ in all his offices (see *WSB* 736). When Wesley gave directions to his preachers for their sermons, he warned against preaching a too limited view of Christ, reducing the rich experience of Christ to a few pat slogans. (Oh, that Wesley would preach to us reductionistic, sloganeering preachers today!)

The modern world tends to love reduced, simple definitions of truth—"the essence of . . . ," "the basic meaning of . . . ," "the essential truth about . . ." Jesus Christ—although the incarnate Son of the living God resists this sort of modernistic simplification. I love the way that Wesleyan theology is determined to find a way to say, to sing, and to serve Jesus Christ that is as rich, as complex, and as dynamic as Jesus Christ. Too often, in the interest of evangelism or reaching the unchurched, or winning converts, we contemporary preachers reduce the gospel to its lowest common denominator, some three-step plan, a series of simple platitudes, and preach that as gospel. Wesley would have a fit.

Once again, poetry says it best. In the "Hymn to the Son," Jesus is displayed in his multifarious offices. Jesus is a Prophet (who tells us the truth about God and ourselves), a Savior (who rescues us from our self-imposed disaster), a Priest (who intercedes for us before the altar of God), a King (who reigns with a mighty hand), and even a Lamb (who is slain but who now rules):

> 6. Prophet, to me reveal
>   Thy Father's perfect will.
>   Never mortal spake like thee,
>   Human prophet like divine;
>   Loud and strong their voices be,
>   Small and still and inward thine!
> 7. On thee my priest I call,
>   Thy blood aton'd for all.
>   Still the Lamb as slain appears,
>   Still thou stand'st before the throne,
>   Ever off'ring up my pray'rs,
>   *These* presenting with thy own.
> 8. Jesu! Thou art my King,
>   From thee my strength I bring!
>   Shadow'd by thy mighty hand,
>   Saviour, who shall pluck me thence?
>   Faith supports, by faith I stand
>   Strong as thy omnipotence. (*HSP* [1739], 110)

In his sermon "The Scripture Way of Salvation," Wesley said that when we receive Christ, "we receive him in all his offices." The great challenge is to do justice to the breadth and depth of Christ's work. (Note that the sidebar "Offices of Christ" is found in the Psalms section, Israel's hymnal section, of the *WSB* 736.)

Something we must not think, if we think about Jesus with Wesley, is that Christ's work is an event of only historical significance. What Christ did on the cross was of decisive significance. On the cross, in the Resurrection, something decisive and final was done about our God problem. But that work was the beginning of our journey with God, not its ending. Christ "died for our sins in accordance with the scriptures" and lives now, works now, for us, in us, and through us, sometimes in spite of us. Although Christ's righteousness on the cross pardoned our sin, his righteous work does not remove the need for our righteousness. Christ's holiness enables us, through the work of his Holy Spirit, to become holy (see *WSB* 828).

THE REIGN OF CHRIST

To affirm that one of the primary offices of Christ is King is to make a claim about the sovereignty of Christ here and now. The poetic prophet Isaiah said that a king will come who will be a servant (not the way we usually think of kings). In that day a new administration of the

Servant will rule the whole wide world. Nations, source of much violence, will at last be at peace. The whole earth will be transformed in God's great ecological restoration. The wild, desiccated desert shall blossom. Wolves will lie peacefully with lambs, wild leopards cavort with young goats, and "a little child shall lead them." The earth will be "full" of the true knowledge of God, like the waters of the sea (Isa. 11:1-9). And a little child will be in charge. After people got to know Jesus, they recalled this text, linking it to his curious sovereignty.

A major way of getting rid of Jesus is to keep him as a distant spiritual possibility. When the Jesus who once was relegated to the realm of a historical figure or a fuzzy spiritual feeling takes up room, stakes out a claim, and becomes the demanding Sovereign One standing beside you, commanding you here and now, well . . .

"What is God's reign like?" Jesus asked as lead-in to many parables. "It is like a mustard seed that someone took and sowed in the garden; it grew and became a tree, and the birds of the air made nests in its branches" (Luke 13:18-19). The kingdom of God is not the result of earnest human effort; it is what God does. God's triumph comes, as surely as harvest follows seedtime. And yet the Kingdom comes surprisingly, starting out ridiculously small, growing by degrees into a "tree." (Actually, mustard is more of a shrub than a tree, a weed, to tell the truth—what we regard as a mere weed, Jesus admires as a glorious tree.)

The Wesleyan movement stressed both God's power active on earth and God's empowerment of ordinary women and men to be agents of God's sovereignty. Though Jesus' talk of gaining a kingdom by working through a little gaggle of disciples or through the sweet older folks who gather in his name at St. John's on the Expressway may seem ridiculous, it is through such preposterously small measures that God miraculously grows a cosmic Kingdom.

When will this Kingdom come? When shall Christ's reign be fully realized? While Wesley anticipated a soon return of Christ to claim his Kingdom, he stressed, like Paul, that there was no need to be sitting around and waiting; we need to be busy as signs and signals of that Kingdom here and now. The Methodist movement itself was claimed as visible proof that a once accustomed, secure world had ended and the promised transformation of the world had already begun. An old world was losing its grip; a new world is being born. Though the Kingdom is not fully, completely come, there's enough of the Kingdom to live with joy and transformed lives right now. Yet the fullness of the reign is still to come so Christians live with the eager expectation that more is yet to come.

Few Wesleyan Christians have worried much about the precise date for that complete transformation. Jesus squelched such speculation by saying, "About that day or hour no one knows, neither the angels in heaven, nor the Son, but only the Father" (Mark 13:32). Most Christians believe that they have had glimpses of the outbreak of the Kingdom on many Sundays in the gathering of the church around God's table or in works of love and mercy in the world. Anytime that God's will is done on earth, it's as if we're seeing visible confirmation of our prayer, "Thy kingdom come, thy will be done, on earth as it is in heaven."

Jesus opened his most famous sermon by announcing a topsy-turvy world, a transformed world, a world quite different from present arrangements:

> Blessed are you who are poor,
>   for yours is the kingdom of God.
> Blessed are you who are hungry now,
>   for you will be filled.
> Blessed are you who weep now,
>   for you will laugh. (Luke 6:20-21)

I like to think that the historic Methodist emphasis on conversion and transformation—both personal and social— is related to our deep and abiding conviction that Jesus shall reign. "Your kingdom come!" (Matt. 6:10; Luke 11:2-4), Jesus taught his disciples always to pray (see *WSB* 1208). Jesus' answer was not to a question like, "How can I have a more purposeful life?" Rather, Jesus as Lord leads people to ask, "How can I get my life aligned with God's purposes for creation?" Jesus' ethics, his way in the world, was not a means of getting into the Kingdom—behave in this way and, if you perform well, someday you will be worthy to enter the Kingdom. The basis of his moral teaching is, "This is reality now that God's kingdom has come and is coming among you, here and now. Wake up. Live in the light of the facts of life."

> Jesus as Lord leads us to ask, "How can I align my purpose with God's?"

The good news, particularly in the Wesleyan idiom, is that we don't have to wait until his reign is obvious to enjoy the revolution (see *WSB* 1357). By forgiving enemies, by blessing those who persecute us, and by taking up the cross daily, we are not called by Jesus to be pious doormats for the world. Rather, we are taking charge in Jesus' name, joining the revolution, beginning the great turnaround toward reality that shall one day be hailed as "the kingdom of the world has become the kingdom of our Lord" in which "he will reign forever and ever" (Rev. 11:15). The life of Jesus leads us to ask "political" questions such as, "Who sits on the throne? Who rules at the very center of heaven?" The answer: a slaughtered, bleeding Lamb who has taken away the sins of the world. That's a King and a Kingdom quite different from the ersatz kingdoms of this world.

In Luke, Jesus' last words from the cross were, "Father, into your hands I commend my spirit" (23:46). Jesus was commending all that he did and all that he said into the hands of God. God's kingdom comes, as Jesus taught, by the action of God. It appears to be the nature of God's kingdom to win victory through suffering, sacrificial love, God weaving into God's purposes, even the worst of human sin, even the sin of crucifying God's own Son. We're not far from the Kingdom whenever we commend our lives and our deeds to God.

I regularly teach a college class on Jesus. During the first class I ask students to write a brief paper on the theme "Who Is Jesus?" The majority of the papers say that "Jesus died to save me from my sins and enable me to go to heaven one day." Some speak of Jesus as "my friend," and a couple say that Jesus is "my Lord." All of these answers are right, as far as they go. But the Wesleyan in me insists that Jesus means even more.

As a preacher, when I read Wesley's long, closely reasoned, sparsely illustrated, doctrinally rich sermons, I marvel at his apparent lack of desire to simplify or to reduce the Christian faith to suit the limitations of his hearers. The sermons are amazingly (sometimes exasperatingly) thick, heavy, tight, and unlike many sermons I preach or I hear today—*theological*. In the current age most of us preachers—in the interest of evangelism or reaching the unchurched, or being culturally relevant—use all sorts of artful devices and slogans to make Jesus more simple, comprehensible, and accessible than Scripture presents Jesus.

Wesley would have none of this, not because he wanted to make it all complicated and difficult but because his desire in preaching was to "offer Christ" (see *WSB* 1347). Wesley's sermons remind us that there's just no way to make salvation in Jesus Christ the subject of our sermons and at the same time speak in undemanding, easily comprehended, and quickly accessible ways. Wesley didn't just want to offer Christ in some reduced, available way, but sought to present Christ as Christ is fully, effusively presented in Scripture. Wesley didn't offer Jesus to the world as a quick fix; he offered Jesus as converter, a transformer of our whole lives and all of creation.

So if at this point, after thinking about Wesleyan thought about Christ and his work, you are beginning to feel your head ache from theological overload, take it up with Wesley! Any theology less conjunctive, less demanding, and less richly biblical wouldn't be worthy of the living Christ who met John Wesley.

CHAPTER THREE

WE BELIEVE IN THE WORK OF THE HOLY SPIRIT

At Pentecost we gathered, Jews from every nation on earth, to remember the gift of the first five books of the Bible to Israel (thus the name for the festival, *penta*= "five"; see Acts 2). No sooner had we gathered to look back in memory than there was the sound "like the rush of a violent wind" that came "suddenly from heaven," and we found our foundations shaken, disrupted, and the Holy Spirit descending, moving us forward. Everybody began to testify to what God was doing in our midst; everybody heard one another speak in spite of our national differences. We had gathered to remember the past, only to have the Holy Spirit thrust us into a new, unexpected future.

This is rather typical behavior for the Holy Spirit, the third person of the Trinity. Just as the Spirit (the "wind from

God") brooded over the waters at Creation, bringing forth life where there had been little but darkness and death (Gen. 1:2), so the Holy Spirit descended at Pentecost bringing forth a new people, the church. The Holy Spirit appears to love to create, to initiate, and to bring something new out of something old, to give possibility and potentiality in times and places where it was thought that we had reached a dead end. Creation, empowerment, speaking and hearing, and yes, even disruption of our placid present with lively, unexpected future—all are typical deeds of the Holy Spirit (see *WSB* 1035).

Thus the same Spirit who hovered over the dark waters at Creation got the story of Jesus started by descending upon Jesus at his baptism "like a dove," saying, "You are my Son, the Beloved; with you I am well pleased" (Mark 1:10-11). (Interestingly, when Matthew told of Jesus' baptism, Matthew implied that the "Spirit of God" descended "like a dove and [alighted] on him" and the voice "from heaven" addressed everyone standing there [Matt. 3:16-17].) It is of the nature of the Holy Spirit to reveal, to speak to us intimately, personally in the depths of our hearts, and to address us publicly, principally through preaching. Thus whenever we read Scripture in our worship, it is typical to pray a Prayer for Illumination that calls upon God to "open our hearts and minds by the power of your Holy Spirit so that as the word is read and proclaimed we may hear what you have to say to us today."

Because the Holy Spirit is a member of the Trinity, that is, God, the Holy Spirit enables us truly to encounter Christ in our reading of Scripture (see *WSB* 1484). The Holy Spirit produces Scripture, enlightens our reading and hearing of Scripture, and enables us to perform Scripture. Miraculously, when we read Scripture, Christ stands among us, present through our reading and hearing of mere words.

What text did Wesley cite as he moved beyond parochial boundaries and preached from the highways and byways glad tidings to the poor? Luke 4:18-19. (See *WSB* 154.) Why did he move from the comfort of the established church's pulpits and placid congregations out to the rough-and-tumble of field preaching? Wesley attributed it to the machinations of the Holy Spirit: "The Spirit of the Lord is upon me to preach good news to the poor" (author paraphrase).

Note how often Jesus is said to be filled and empowered, prompted by and speaking from the Holy Spirit in this favorite Wesleyan passage from Luke's Gospel:

> Jesus, full of the Holy Spirit, returned from the Jordan and was led by the Spirit in the wilderness. . . . Then Jesus, filled with the power of the Spirit, returned to Galilee, and a report about him spread through all the surrounding country. He began to teach in their synagogues and was praised by everyone. When he came to Nazareth, where he had been brought up, he went to the synagogue on the sabbath day, as was his

custom. He stood up to read, and the scroll of the prophet Isaiah was given to him. He unrolled the scroll and found the place where it was written:

"The Spirit of the Lord is upon me,

because he has anointed me

to bring good news to the poor." (Luke 4:1, 14-18a)

The Holy Spirit tells Christians what to think about God and how to speak to and for God. Paul said that though we don't always know just how to pray, the Holy Spirit helps us. Jesus told his disciples that when they haul you into a courtroom (note that he didn't say *if* they arrest you and throw you in the slammer but *when* they arrest you), don't plan your defense speeches to the court in advance: "When they bring you before the synagogues, the rulers, and the authorities, do not worry about how you are to defend yourselves or what you are to say; for the Holy Spirit will teach you at that very hour what you ought to say" (Luke 12:11-12).

That's why, when Scripture is read or a sermon is preached, we often pray, "Lord, open our hearts and minds by the power of your Holy Spirit so that we can hear what you want to say to us today," or words to that effect. The Holy Spirit is a great

> **The Holy Spirit tells us what to think about God and how to speak for God.**

teacher, telling us things we could never come up with on our own. Just as Jesus preached in "the power of the Spirit" in Nazareth (Luke 4:14), so Jesus' Holy Spirit enables us to speak about Jesus and to hear Jesus. Even faith in Jesus is a gift of Jesus in the power of the Spirit. As Paul put it, "No one can say 'Jesus is Lord' except by the Holy Spirit" (1 Cor. 12:3).

It is not an exaggeration to say that the Wesleyan doctrine of the Holy Spirit is our distinctive emphasis in our appropriation of orthodox Christian theology. Pneumatology (*pneuma*, Greek for "wind" that is also rendered "spirit" or "breath" in the New Testament) accounts for why United Methodists have not been into biblical fundamentalism. We have too much respect for the thickness and largeness of Scripture to reduce the bubbling vitality of the Bible to a set of fundamentals. More than that, we are deeply convinced that Scripture is the grand arena of the Holy Spirit. Scripture is always more than the letter that is fixed and final on the page. Scripture is—by the grace of the Holy Spirit—a lively, speaking presence among us, prodding us, summoning us, pulling us toward God, enlarging our notions of God. No abstract, reduced fundamentals, no matter how long a list we could come up with, can say as much to us as the Holy Spirit.

So in United Methodist lore we all know the story of John Wesley, priggish little Oxford don who ran hither and thither, working, praying, studying, traveling as a would-be

> I trust in Christ, Christ alone, for salvation. He takes away *my* sins, even *mine*.

missionary to the heathens in Georgia, only to be blindsided by God's reassuring grace while at (of all places) a church meeting on Aldersgate Street in London on May 24, 1738. There, quite apart from all that Wesley had been doing for God, the Holy Spirit did something to Wesley. Wesley discovered at Aldersgate that the God for whom he had been so relentlessly searching was, in truth, searching for him. He was found by the ever-seeking Spirit. John Wesley wrote in his journal that his heart was "strangely warmed," not by just any heartwarming sentiment but by the assurance that "I did trust in Christ, Christ alone, for salvation . . . that he had taken away *my* sins, even *mine*, and saved *me* from the law of sin and death" (May 24, 1738).

Wesley's statement about Aldersgate in his journal is clearly, classically Protestant: justification (pardon, forgiveness) of sinful humanity by the work of Jesus on the cross and in resurrection. The new stress that Wesley gave to such classical belief was its appropriation in the life of the believer, the experience of assurance of that justification (the "witness of the Spirit" as he called it). And this is why Wesleyans tend to stress the delightfulness and the necessity of heartwarming experiences of God's love—conversion (see *WSB* 1446), regeneration (see *WSB* 1115), and new birth (see *WSB* 1289)—as pneumatological gifts of a most determined Holy Spirit (see *WSB* 1368).

GRACE IN THREE WAYS

Prevenient Grace

For Wesleyans, our chief evidence of the character and the reality of the Holy Spirit is grace (see *WSB* 1428). The Greek word in the New Testament that is translated as "grace" (*charis*) means simply "gift." Our relationship to Christ is instituted by his gift of himself, and it is sustained through countless gifts of love that generate, through the Holy Spirit, gracious, holy living (see *WSB* 180, 290, 1110). We exist with God—Father, Son, and Holy Spirit—every moment of our lives, every step of our life's way, only by gift, solely by grace.

Grace is an often misunderstood Wesleyan concept (see *WSB* 1110). Too many of us think of grace in a sentimental, unbiblical way—grace as the unmerited present given to us from God, a present that we are at liberty to take or to refuse. Or grace is vaguely conceived as a substance, a saccharine ooze that is spread over all of life's ills and our shortcomings that makes everything sweeter than it really is.

Grace, particularly as it is described and lived in the Wesleyan tradition, is relational—God relating to us in ways that are enlightening, transforming, and empowering (see *WSB* 1110). Grace is the God-given ability to lead a different life. Grace is the God-given ability to live for God rather than, as comes most naturally, for ourselves. Thus Wesleyans speak of growth in grace in much the same way that we speak of growth in a friendship with someone (see *WSB* 1480). Just as friendship between people takes time, feeds upon shared good times and bad, deepens with each mutual challenge and hurdle, gives gifts and receives gifts, so our friendship with God. The Christian life is not often an instantaneous full relationship with God. More typically for us Wesleyans, the Christian life is a long process of being drawn gradually closer into God and out of ourselves, all by the workings of God's grace in us.

True to our propensity toward conjunctive theology, we Wesleyans speak of the triune God's loving work with us, grace in three ways: as prevenient grace *and* justifying grace *and* sanctifying grace. *Prevenient grace* is God's love coming to us even before we are consciously aware that it is God's love (see *WSB* 605). Prevenient grace (literally, "coming before") is the strange but wonderful way that God intrudes into each life, convincing us of our need, awakening us to God's presence and gracious availability to us, convicting us of our sin and our need for God, prophetically telling us the truth about ourselves, and lovingly leading us to repentance, gradually, often imperceptibly turning us from preoccupation with self and toward enthusiasm to do the will of God. Prevenient grace tells us the truth that we are incapable of telling to ourselves (see *WSB* 690), strangely empowering us to be better for God than we could have been had we been on our own.

> **Prevenient grace is God's mysterious testimony to us that we are not, never have been, and never will be on our own.**

Prevenient grace is God's mysterious testimony to us that we are not, never have been, and never will be on our own. We are not left to our own devices when it comes to our relationship with God. God doesn't wait for us but graciously makes the first moves toward us. We are not alone. Thus prevenient grace is our experience of God's determination (seen most vividly in the cross and resurrection of Jesus, but continuing subtly, powerfully in our daily experiences of God's love) to be in relationship with us. Alas, many of us North Americans tend to think of religion in personal, private, individual terms rather than in social, communal, relational terms. Religion is something nice that we do every now and then for God rather than primarily, preveniently what God is constantly, busily doing in us. We think of our search for God when, in truth, God searches for us and finds us, despite our efforts to flee. We think of our worship as our acts of love toward God rather than see our worship, our lives, and our relationship to God as God's activity toward and in us. In our sin we can never aspire to God; God must condescend to us. God is always the antecedent, the prior condition, the necessary first step for any relationship we have with God, the power that enables any responsiveness from us. As Jesus said, "You didn't choose me; I chose you that you should go and bear fruit in my name" (John 15:16, author translation).

God's prevenient grace, coming to us before we know it as God's grace, is a disarming reminder that our lives are not our own. In that regard prevenient grace is proof of the atoning (at-one-ment) work of Jesus Christ. There is something about a trinitarian God who constantly works a way toward us, despite us.

The Holy Spirit refused to let John Wesley's sincere but often priggish and soulless piety get in the way of God's making a way to John Wesley that evening at Aldersgate Street. Wesley thought he was going to a church meeting, only to be blindsided by an unexpected meeting with God. Let this be a lesson to you: if you are going to be in relationship with a living God, a God who works preveniently, then don't be surprised that often you will be surprised.

Justifying Grace

Wesleyans name the accepting, pardoning love that meets us in Jesus and his cross and resurrection and the decisive change that comes when we are given an awareness of that redeeming work as *justifying grace*.

Scripture—Old Testament and New—is a story of undeserved, unmerited, unexpected grace, of new beginnings and a fresh start that is given by God. I find it interesting how many Wesleyan Core Term sidebars related to grace and its workings are found in the Old Testament of the *WSB*. This is a fine reminder that it is wrong to say something simplistic like, "The Old Testament is a collection of books on law and judgment, and the New Testament is a collection of writings on love and grace." When Wesleyans read Scripture, we read all of Scripture, and we tend to see grace everywhere. The same God, who, through the Son, worked the world's redemption, was busy working redemption in Jacob, Moses, Miriam, and Ruth before it was worked in Peter, Paul, Mary, and Lydia. The God who encountered people on the bank of the river Jabbok also met them beside the river Jordan.

For Wesleyans it's never enough simply to say, "God is love." We must also note that God is redeeming, justifying love, love in action, love on the move toward us. When we Christians talk about *justification*, we mean that we have been assured, through the Holy Spirit's vivification of the truth of this story in our lives, that in Jesus Christ, God was doing something decisive about our sad situation (see *WSB* 1480). In word processing, we justify the margins of text, bringing all the text into line. So in Jesus Christ, we who were once out of line with God were brought back in line through the loving work of God (see *WSB* 1073). We who were nobodies became somebodies. We who had no future with God because of our sin and rebellion were given a tomorrow. We who had wandered into a far country (Luke 15) were sought, found, saved, and brought back from the dead. Few walk away from a true encounter with this story, this cross, this shock and surprise of God with us, without being totally new people. And this too is all grace.

Thus the experience of justifying grace is often spoken of as our *conversion*. We delight (in Wesley's way of putting this) in the gift of "new birth" (see *WSB* 1522). New birth is a total makeover wrought by God's grace in us. Wesleyans enjoy Spirit-induced decisive breaks with the hackneyed old and a resolute entrance into the creative and the novel. As we have noted, it is of the nature of the Holy Spirit to begin things, to make something out of nothing, and to offer possibility. Yet when thinking about conversion, we Wesleyans tend not to think of conversion (as some American evangelicals have thought) as only an instantaneous, one-time event. For us, transforming grace tends to be experienced as a long process of transformation, of gradual growth in grace, in which innumerable experiences of God's saving grace fit into a process of the larger whole, sanctification.

You already know that one rarely becomes a really good friend of anyone overnight. Friendship takes time—long walks together, meandering conversations, time spent just hanging out. So it is with our friendship with God. We believe that moving on to perfection (that is, attaining

God-given maturity and complete wholeness in God) tends to be lifelong. We rarely get so mature in the faith, so perfected and holy, that God has no more growing for us to do. (More about that shortly when we discuss that dear Wesleyan focus, sanctification.)

Wesley stressed an assurance of salvation (see *WSB* 1523). The church exists joyfully to proclaim that in Christ, God was and is "reconciling the world to himself" (2 Cor. 5:19). This is an accomplished fact that is continuing to be accomplished in our lives through the work of the Holy Spirit. We are able to love God boldly because, in Christ, God has first boldly loved us. We need not spend our lives with God anxiety-ridden, full of consternation and caution, worried about just where we stand with God. We don't need constantly to be taking our spiritual temperatures, relentlessly scanning every step that we take, troubled that we may have messed up so badly that God will at last give up on us. We know whose we are. We believe that God does not let go of those lives for which God in Christ has so dearly paid. We believe that we really know God because God has fully known us. Wesley loved to cite Romans 8:15-16: "When we cry, 'Abba! Father!' it is that very Spirit bearing witness with our spirit that we are children of God." We are thus assured of God's resourceful, adopting love for us as God's Holy Spirit connects with our spirits, assuring us of where we stand with God.

Wesley spoke of the "witness of the Spirit" (Sermon 10), echoing Romans 8:16, in which he celebrated the Holy Spirit's "bearing witness with our spirit that we are children of God." A loving God does not leave us without confirmation and assurance that we are loved and accepted as God's own. In stressing the witness of the Spirit, Wesley joined personal spiritual experience to the traditional Anglican stress on reason, Scripture, and tradition as an important means of discernment in matters of faith (see *WSB* 851). Experience was not a matter of what seems right to me, certainly not a matter of some stirring but short-lived feeling. Rather, it was experience of a living God, through the power of the Holy Spirit, working in us to say to us what we cannot say to ourselves.

And how do we know that our assurance is not merely our self-assurance? Wesley stressed the marks of salvation, the visible "fruits of the Spirit" (see *WSB* 1429) and "marks of new birth" (see *WSB* 1522). If there is spiritual fruit, evidence, results, then there is spiritual assurance. For Wesley this was a widely attested, obvious scriptural truth: disciples want to look, act, and talk like their Master. The more we obey the Master, the closer we servants come to the Master. As we reach out to the world in the name of the Christ who has reached out to us, we find ourselves being drawn ever closer to the love of Christ. A Christian is someone who, at least to some visible degree, actually walks and talks like Jesus because he or she intimately, personally knows Jesus.

Sanctifying Grace

Our wonder at God's gracious justification of humanity is matched by God's amazing work through *sanctifying grace*. The purpose of the myriad laws that God gave to Israel was to sanctify Israel, to make Israel God's set-apart people who would be "a priestly kingdom and a holy nation" (Exod. 19:6). In Israel, the world would see what God could do with ordinary people who were transformed by God's extraordinary grace. As Wesley put the relationship of prevenient, justifying, and sanctifying grace: "Our main doctrines, which include all the rest, are three, that of repentance, of faith, and of holiness. The first of these we account, as it were, the porch of religion; the next, the door; the third is religion itself" ("The Principles of a Methodist Farther Explained," §VI.4; see *WSB* 149). Thus using this porch, door, house metaphor, we tend to think of prevenient grace as the porch whereby we are drawn toward Christ, justifying grace as the door that Christ opens to us, and then the many-roomed house (John 14:2) in which we are invited to explore and to dwell for all eternity in full sanctification, "religion itself."

If grace is a distinctive Wesleyan emphasis, then sanctifying grace is the most distinctive aspect of the Wesleyan view of grace. God not only does something for us in our justification in the cross and resurrection of Jesus, but God continues actively to work in us in constantly drawing us nearer, in continually making us more loving and faithful, and empowering us to be better disciples—sanctifying grace.

In affirming sanctification as strongly as justification, Wesley parted company with aspects of traditional Lutheran and Calvinistic teaching on justification. The disagreement tended to be about a differing conception of humanity before and after the gracious work of God. Lutherans stressed that we are, even after justification, fully justified but still fully sinful, sinful and saintly at the same time. We don't stop being sinful just because we are justified by Christ on the cross. In the Reformed tradition (Calvin and his heirs) there is a constant struggle with sin, and whatever victories we have over sin tend to be temporary. We never stop needing the grace and forgiveness of the Savior who died for sinners.

Wesley tended to agree with both Lutherans and Calvinists on these points yet differed on sanctification. He taught the dangerous idea (in the judgment of his Lutheran and Reformed critics) that while our sin is deep and serious, God's grace is even more powerful. God imparts righteousness to converted sinners, whereby we actually become holy, being freed from the power as well as the guilt of sin, and having the possibility (though not necessarily probability) of living without committing conscious, voluntary, knowing sins (being totally saturated with love of God and neighbor). In short, by the grace of God, we can genuinely grow in grace. We can actually be more holy and faithful than we were when we first turned to Christ.

The same Holy Spirit who brooded over the waters at Creation and brought forth new life brings forth new life in us as well (see *WSB* 1414). Wesley adhered closely to the original Greek in his translation of 2 Corinthians 5:17: "If *any one* be in Christ, *there* is a new creation" (*Notes*). Then he added in commentary, "Only the power that makes a world can make a Christian." The sanctification of a sinner is a miracle on the same level as the miraculous creation of the cosmos. The transformative, darkness-to-light power of the love of God is seen nowhere more dramatically than in a sinner like you or me sanctified, commandeered by the love of God in Christ.

Wesley, whose own heartwarming assurance at Aldersgate demonstrated the gifted quality of justification by faith alone, was never able to preach just faith alone. To faith he added—as confirmation of and stimulus to faith—sanctifying spiritual disciplines, practices, sacraments, and good works (see *WSB* 884, 1308). Claims of justification without evidence of sanctification were what Wesley called "dead religion." If one neglected good works toward God and neighbor, Wesley thought that it was possible, indeed probable, to "backslide," to forfeit the good work of God in you by neglecting good works for God. Use it or lose it was Wesley's view of grace.

In a sermon on the work of the Holy Spirit in us, Wesley said: "By 'the grace of God' is sometimes to be understood that free love, that unmerited mercy, by which I, a sinner, through the merits of Christ am now reconciled to God. But in this place it rather means that power of God the Holy Ghost which 'worketh in us both to will and to do of his good pleasure'" (Sermon 12, "The Witness of Our Own Spirit," §15).

To those who charged Wesley with that dreaded Protestant anathema "salvation by works," he countered that any good work we do, before or after justification, is due to the grace of God working in us through the Holy Spirit. Faith without good works is not really biblical faith, for faith is always known in Scripture by its ability to produce, even among foul sinners like us, truly good fruit. Wesley thus refused to contrast faith with good works. The two go together like love and marriage, or faith is not faith and our works are not really good. By the sanctifying grace of God, we are sanctified, made holy, so that for the first time in our lives we are free actually to do something good for God and neighbor. By the gracious disciplining of our lives to God, our lives are healed and made more true to God's originating intentions for us. To our surprise and delight, we wake up to find ourselves miraculously moving in the same direction as God, working with the grain of the universe because God is working in and through us. We are startled to find that we want what God wants, and our desire is gradually consumed by a desire for God's will to be done on earth as it is in heaven.

Wesley found a way to avoid the Reformation tendency to contrast "faith alone" with "holy living." *Conjunctive theology* (two seemingly different theological ideas joined by *and*) is what we earlier named as this Wesleyan tendency to join two theological assertions that were otherwise kept rather separate and distinct. He combined classical Augustinian affirmations (a strong sense of original sin, a vivid appreciation for the sovereignty of God) with a joyful Christian ethic of human responsiveness that sometimes sounds almost Eastern Orthodox in its blissful celebration of the restoration of the once defaced image of God in us. In his evangelistic message Wesley joined justification and regeneration with sanctification, avoiding both vaunted human self-assertion and human ethical passivity in the face of God's sovereign salvation of us.

Confidence in the power of the Holy Spirit to overcome all of our self-imposed resistance, to construct true Christians out of the stuff of us sinners, makes the work of the Holy Spirit the engine that drives all Wesleyan theology. The Holy Spirit is not exotic, optional equipment for a Christian. We depend on the Holy Spirit as much as we depend on air. In fact, John Wesley spoke of "spiritual respiration" (see *WSB* 753) to emphasize the necessity of being constantly connected to the Holy Spirit. (See Sermon 45, "The New Birth," §II.4.) Like air filling our lungs, the spirit of God fills our lives, making us refreshed and ready to do God's work. Stop breathing God and our spiritual lives wilt.

Because our spiritual respiration is not involuntary, unlike our natural breathing, we must concentrate on being receptive to the Holy Spirit through prayer and the sacraments, Bible study, and other spiritual practices that assist us in cultivating life in the Spirit.

It is the nature of the Holy Spirit to work through a multitude of means to make God present to us, to give us not only the presence of God to us but also the power of God working in us.

Thus I met two older women who have begun and sustained a ministry within one of our local jails for youthful offenders. They visit twice a week and volunteer to teach literacy courses to the inmates. They also make sure that every young man's birthday is celebrated with a cake and presents provided by local United Methodist churches.

"I have really surprised myself," said one of the women. "I've always been a rather shy person, not the type to venture out and attempt new things. Can you believe what God has done for these young men through someone like me?"

It was, for me, a wonderfully Wesleyan testimonial to the effects of the Holy Spirit. I guess the wild story in Acts 2 is true.

CHAPTER FOUR

WE BELIEVE IN THE GUIDANCE OF SCRIPTURE

W e would know nothing about the Trinity, redemption in Jesus, or the work of grace through the Holy Spirit if God had not given us Scripture. Christian doctrine is a product of the church's encounter with a group of ancient writings that were compiled over a four-thousand-year period, none of which are younger than nearly two thousand years. The church is sustained, encouraged, and at the

> In our encounters with Scripture we believe we hear the voice, see the ways, and receive the guidance of the living God.

same time severely criticized and challenged by the very same Scripture that the church produced. We meet Christ in Scripture in a way that is singular and fecund. In our encounters with Scripture we believe we hear the voice, see the ways, and receive the guidance of the living God.

Scripture was produced by communities of faith who had experienced God's presence and interaction with them in vivid ways. Something undeniable and real had happened to them, and now they wanted to tell everyone the news. Not that all their testimony was uniform or rendered in the same way. In fact, some of the diversity of the testimony is a sort of proof that the events they were trying to relate were so mind-boggling and boundary-breaking that they were very difficult to put into speech. We are the beneficiaries of their testimony; we are the result of the encounter that their testimony provokes in each succeeding generation:

> We declare to you . . . , what we have heard, what we have seen . . . , what we have . . . touched with our hands, concerning the word of life. . . . We declare to you what we have seen and heard so that you also may have fellowship with us; and truly our fellowship is with the Father and with his Son Jesus Christ. We are writing these things so that our joy may be complete. (1 John 1:1-4)

It is a principle of faithful Christian doctrine that we try hard to make no theological statement that does not arise out of and is in turn answerable to Scripture. In theology, ideas and concepts that can claim no other source than fertile human imagination are otherwise known as heresy—God talk that originates in ourselves rather than in Scripture. That's one reason why after the Articles of Religion speak of God—Father, Son, and Holy Spirit—the very next topic is "Of the Sufficiency of the Holy Scriptures for Salvation" (Article 5, *BOD*), a statement that claims that the Bible "containeth all things necessary to salvation." Lest you think of theology as a complicated affair, something that you can never hope to figure out, Article 5 reassures you that everything anyone really needs to know in order to be with God is graciously given in the Bible (see *WSB* 1288). We need not rummage around elsewhere for revelation. It's all here, more than we'll ever be able to process in a lifetime of sermons, all that we need to know of God and more.

Today, when popular novels and movies come forth claiming to have exposed some secret knowledge, a story of some sinister church plot that has now been revealed, it's good to know that, while such claims sometimes make for a good story, the church loves us enough to reassure us that there are not two classes of Christians—those who have been let in on the secret knowledge and those benighted souls who have yet to find the hidden key. All struggling believers are reassured: God's revelation is not rare, arcane, and obtuse. What God is doing for us and what God promises us and what God expects of us, all is fully revealed in Scripture.

Of course, if you have read much of Scripture, our saying that the Bible contains "all things necessary to salvation" does not mean that Christian theology, based on God's revelation that comes through Scripture, is thereby simple or self-evident. One reason why you are reading this book, correlating theology with Scripture, is that you know that God's word in Scripture requires humble listening, informed discernment, and prayerful searching.

SEARCHING THE SCRIPTURES

In the previous chapter we discussed the primacy of the grace of God as God's loving work among us. John Wesley listed "searching the Scriptures" as one of the primary instituted *means of grace*, right up there with other sacramental means of grace like the Eucharist and baptism. Against all fuzzy notions of grace in the contemporary church, Wesley's searching of Scripture as a means of grace gives grace content, substance, and intellectual clout. As a lifelong student of Scripture, Wesley boasted of being a "man of one book," reading the Bible in the original languages, showing a deep knowledge of both Hebrew and Greek in his notes on the Bible (see *WSB* 744). Methodism, born on the Oxford University campus, has not been threatened by study of Scripture in its original languages. From the beginning Wesley insisted that his preachers be educated, in spite of whatever formal educational limitations they may have, by being steeped in the Bible, constantly growing through constant interaction with the sacred text (see *WSB* 997).

The expression *means of grace* indicates that true understanding of the riches of Scripture requires the loving intervention of God—you can't read Scripture by yourself at home or even in a college Bible class; you need the Holy Spirit to enlighten and enliven the word from the printed page. Reading and comprehending the Bible are acts of prayer.

Yet *searching the Scriptures* is an expression that also denotes the need for active, earnest work in wrestling with the ancient text until it blesses us with revelation. Once again we encounter Wesley's conjunctive theology—Scripture reading and understanding require the gift of God's revelation coupled with our

> Yet *searching the Scriptures* is an expression that also denotes the need for active, earnest work in wrestling with the ancient text until it blesses us with revelation.

determined, intellectually responsible and responsive work.

The United Methodist *Book of Discipline* continues this tradition with its affirmation of the need for careful, prayerful, informed discernment in our reading of Scripture:

We are aided by scholarly inquiry and personal insight, under the guidance of the Holy Spirit. As we work with each text, we take into account what we have been able to learn about the original context and intention of that text. In this understanding we draw upon the careful historical, literary, and textual studies of recent years, which have enriched our understanding of the Bible. (¶104, "Scripture")

The Wesley Study Bible is a *study* Bible with copious notes at the bottom of every page, not to mention the frequent sidebars. The *WSB* is thus a culmination of the contemporary explosion of study Bibles and aids to biblical study that has blessed the church in recent decades. Scripture is not to be read alone, not only in the sense that we need the descent of the Holy Spirit to make Scripture work, to enable Scripture to speak, but we also need help from our friends who have spent their lives working with Scripture, ferreting out meanings for the ancient text, putting the text in context, and who now share their insights with the rest of us, challenging any of our merely personal, idiosyncratic, and uninformed interpretations.

The books of Ezra and Nehemiah depict Israel's return from the waste of Babylonian exile. During the reconstruction of the wall of Jerusalem, a Torah (the Old Testament books of the Law) scroll was found. God's gracious guidance to Israel had been lost due to the decades of exile in a foreign land. The people assembled and heard the Law read as if for the first time. They wept when they heard the word, weeping for sadness that they had lost the word and had wandered, weeping for joy that at last God's word had rediscovered them again (Neh. 8:1-12). They were home.

This is Israel at its best, a people constituted by little more than a group of ancient writings. Israel, and the church after it, is that peculiar people who are assembled on the basis of Scripture, people who listen, ponder, and align themselves with God's word to them. The *WSB* uses this period in Ezra as occasion for a sidebar on studying Scripture (see *WSB* 576), noting that Wesley (a "man of one book") studied Scripture "both critically and devotionally." Using the riches of church tradition (see *WSB* 1406), his own logic, and relevant contemporary experience, Wesley mined the wealth of Scripture and encouraged all Methodists, even the less educated among them, to "search the Scriptures" too. Devotionally, Wesley stressed that when we read the Bible, we search for the will of God. We are to search not only Scripture but also our own hearts in our listening for God's word, engaging in self-examination, willing to repent of past understandings and grow into fresh experiences of God's presence through Scripture. Our study of Scripture is not merely an intellectual exercise but also a means of prayer, a way to equip ourselves for discipleship.

The *WSB* continues the Wesleyan tradition of dynamic interaction with Scripture. In the *WSB* Paul's first letter to the Corinthians is introduced by telling us that this early congregation was "the most troublesome of his churches" (see *WSB* 1389). It even quotes John Wesley, who wonders how on earth, in a church scarcely a decade or so removed from the death and resurrection of Christ, the "mystery of iniquity" could have worked so fast. Wesley noted the "'schisms' and 'heresies,' animosities, fierce and bitter contentions . . . [and even] fornication" among the Corinthians (Sermon 61, "The Mystery of Iniquity," §18). I wonder if it would take a church reformer like Wesley, caught in the daily tug and pull of fierce contemporary church conflict, to note this deep mystery of iniquity. Do Wesley's notes on First Corinthians remind you of any congregations of your acquaintance? I suppose that those of us who struggle in the contemporary church may take some comfort in discovering the mystery of iniquity a long time ago among the Corinthians.

Then, a couple of pages later, Paul contrasted the "foolishness" of a crucified Savior with the "wisdom" of the world (1 Cor. 1:18-19), referring to the Corinthian congregation, for all their problems, as visible demonstration that "God chose what is foolish in the world to shame the wise . . . so that no one might boast in the presence of God" (1 Cor. 1:27, 29). The *WSB* gives a note at the bottom of the page in which Wesley preached on this text and provides a sidebar on the core term, "Overvaluing of Reason" (see *WSB* 1391).

The sidebar explains that while Wesley, scholar that he was, cherished the use of human reason, he also knew that "reason by itself could never produce faith, hope, and love." Intellectually, Wesley's movement was a wonderful conjunction of scholarly appropriation of Scripture *and* the church's tradition with heartfelt, passionate spirituality. Thus our understanding of Scripture is greatly aided by our friends, some of them long dead, when we read the Bible in conversation with those who have wrestled with the word long before us (see *WSB* 414).

Let's face it, sometimes we search the Scriptures, using our reason (see *WSB* 777), in order to deflect, evade, and avoid Scripture's claim upon our lives! Sometimes we are guilty of searching Scripture in order to confirm our cherished prejudices and to dodge the possibility of new light from God and moral transformation of ourselves. Therefore, Wesley would have us search with humility, expecting surprises in our reading and interpretation, confident that the Holy Spirit wants to enliven Scripture in our hearing, obedient to the vocation of God that we hear within Scripture. Rather than ask of a biblical text, "Do I agree with this?" or say, "That seems about right to me," we ought to ask ourselves, "How would my life have to change in order to show the world that this Scripture is true?" Rather than pleas for intellectual agreement, many passages of Scripture are calls to conversion (see *WSB* 304), an invitation to see firsthand what the grace of God can do in a life.

Thus Paul's stirring claim (2 Cor. 5:17), "If anyone is in Christ, there is a new creation: everything old has passed away; see, everything has become new!" is set alongside the core term "New Creation" (see *WSB* 1414). I love Wesley's commentary on this passage: "Only the power that makes a world can make a Christian" (*Notes*). In speaking of life in Christ as "new creation," Paul connected the present experience of the creation of the church with the ancient testimony from Genesis about the creation of the world. And I love the way Wesley noted that when someone awakens to Christ, it is almost like Genesis 1 all over again. It's nothing less than a whole new world.

THE WHOLE OF SCRIPTURE

Methodists followed the Articles of Religion in affirming the whole of Scripture, both Old and New Testaments: "The Old Testament is not contrary to the New; for both in the Old and New Testament everlasting life is offered to mankind by Christ" (Article 6, *BOD*). While the Bible is a product of human beings' listening for God in diverse times and places, these various witnesses together help us to understand the wonder of our salvation in Jesus Christ (see *WSB* 1282).

Too often the reading of Scripture in modernity has tended to stress the contradictions and the disunity of Scripture. Some modern methods of biblical interpretation, in attempting to peel away the layers of biblical passages, imply that the Scripture that is the closest to our own epoch is the most valuable. Wesley was convinced that Scripture, while undeniably diverse and multivocal, ancient and demanding, has a sort of dynamic unity. The same God who is revealed in the Hebrew Scriptures is revealed in the Jew, Jesus Christ. The grace of God that we see so vividly in Jesus is also present in the witness of Jacob and Joseph. Individual passages must be interpreted in light of the larger whole. When we come across passages that seem contradictory or downright offensive, Wesley said that we need to examine those passages in the light of what he called the "general tenor" or the "whole scope and tenor of Scripture" (Sermon 110, "Free Grace," §§20–23).

We are modern people who have been taught by our culture to believe that we are privileged to stand upon the very summit of human development. From our serene contemporary perch we stand in judgment on everyone who got here before us. We have progressed. We are making progress. We know so much more than they. To affirm that Scripture, "both in the Old and New Testament," is a reliable, unsubstitutable guide for our salvation, our future with God, is to go against modern prejudice. We look for God and listen for God with these ancient witnesses who have gone before us. We do our best to allow the various voices within the canon of Scripture to share their distinctive testimonies with us. Fortunately, we need not reinvent the wheel in regard to Christian discipleship. If we will dare listen, the saints will show us the way.

To say that Scripture ought to be read as a whole puts at rest the unfortunate stereotype that has demeaned the Old Testament, playing it off against the New with slogans such as, "The Old Testament is a collection of laws and judgment; the New Testament contains books of love and grace." Wesley found grace in many parts of the Hebrew Scriptures, and he strongly believed (against some in the Protestant Reformation, that is, Luther) that God's law was a sign of God's gracious, loving determination not to leave us alone to make do with our own devices. He rejected any simplistic or wooden law-versus-gospel distinction.

Wesley therefore taught that it is wrong to lift out of context a single passage of Scripture, attempting to read that passage isolated from other relevant passages. Scripture interprets Scripture and cumulatively points toward God's love and care.

Prooftexting—searching for one passage that proves your pet doctrine or disproves your neighbor's pet doctrine—is an abuse of Scripture's unity and "general tenor" (see *WSB* 1282). All passages of Scripture must be read in the context of the whole story that God is telling us through Scripture. Martin Luther was fond of saying that the Bible is like the swaddling clothes that were wrapped around the baby Jesus, the manger in which Christ was laid. We don't worship the Bible; we worship the Savior to whom all Scripture—in diverse ways—testifies. All Scripture, Old Testament and New, points to and is to be evaluated by the supreme revelation of God, the Incarnate Word—Jesus Christ.

As Jesus told some of his critics: "You search the scriptures because you think that in them you have eternal life; and it is they that testify on my behalf. Yet you refuse to come to me to have life" (John 5:39-40).

I find revealing that the *WSB* places the sidebar about the "Wholeness of Scripture" in the context of the incognito risen Christ and his attempt to open the Scriptures to the two dull disciples on the road to Emmaus (Luke 24:13-31). I'm sure that the editors so placed this sidebar because it relates to the risen Christ's sweeping Bible study that began "with Moses and all the prophets." The risen Christ interpreted the miracle of the Resurrection by reference to the Hebrew Scriptures. And yet, despite Jesus himself doing the Scripture instruction, the disciples understood nothing about the Scriptures until Jesus, with them "at table," blessed, broke, and gave the bread. Only then their "eyes were opened" (24:31), and they saw that the stranger was none other than their Lord and Savior. We need the presence of Christ to understand Scripture. All Scripture ultimately points to the Christ and must finally answer to the revelation of God in Jesus Christ.

SCRIPTURAL HOLINESS

Wesleyan appropriation of Scripture has always desired more than mere intellectual understanding of the Bible. One of Wesley's distinctive contributions to the church's use of Scripture is his teaching that people should expect

that reading the Bible is a primary opportunity to experience the transforming presence and power of God in their
lives. Thus the *WSB* sidebar on "Scriptural Holiness" (see
WSB 255) opens up the ancient rite of circumcision in a
Wesleyan way. Just as circumcision was the means of signifying a Jew as a Jew—someone set apart, claimed by God
as a member of a holy people—so contemporary Christians
are set apart and claimed by God to be holy. Deuteronomy
10:16 says to "circumcise . . . your heart"—be in obedient,
loving relationship with God in the depths of your being—
and "love the LORD your God with all your heart and . . .
soul, in order that you may live" (30:6). Wesley caught up
these Old Testament concepts of holiness in his practice of
scriptural holiness—that transforming, morally formative,
life-giving relationship of reciprocal love between God and
God's people right now, right here, in everything we do.

Whereas in Deuteronomy 10:16 God urges Israel to circumcise their hearts, Deuteronomy 30:6 suggests that God
himself will circumcise them—a very Wesleyan reminder
that any transformation in righteousness, any growth in
holiness and love, is a miraculous work of God's grace. Still,
Wesley would want us to remind ourselves that God's grace
is responsible grace, a gift that evokes our responsible
participation.

Thus the heirs of Wesley have always stressed that Scripture is not merely to be understood, pondered, and debated
but also enacted, embodied, and performed. We are to intellectually understand Scripture and to practically, morally
enact Scripture in our lives. The truth of Scripture is known
in its performance. In the *WSB* when Jesus encountered the

rich man (Mark 10:17-31), the sidebar "Use of Money" (see *WSB* 1223) talks about widespread misunderstanding of Wesley's famous maxim, "Gain all you can . . . save all you can . . . give all you can." In regard to money, Wesley meant to stress not gaining and hoarding all we can but economizing, getting along with the minimum of material possessions and, in short, keeping wealth in its place as much as we can. All study of Scripture is to be validated by enactment of Scripture.

PRACTICE READING

Typical of one who stressed *practical divinity* (Christian belief as meant to be put into practice), Wesley envisioned the reading of Scripture as a matter of exercising a wide array of practices: Wesley's "Large Minutes" explain that Scripture is a means of grace when we search the Scriptures by "reading: <u>Constantly</u>, some part of every day; <u>regularly</u>, all the Bible in order; <u>carefully</u>, with the Notes; <u>seriously</u>, with prayer before and after; <u>fruitfully</u>, immediately practising what you learn there."

> **Read the Scriptures constantly, regularly, carefully, seriously, and fruitfully.**

The Bible is demanding literature, not only because it is ancient literature written in languages other than our own but also because it commands obedience, response, and enactment. Therefore, the Bible requires being read "constantly" and "regularly"—"all" of it. To modern readers, accustomed to rather linear, flat narratives that neatly fit into our limited definitions of reality, the Bible can come across to us as a mess. To be sure, one encounters inconsistencies and contradictions, to say nothing of downright bad ideas in the Bible.

Scripture has a marvelous way of arguing with itself, correcting itself, one witness giving countertestimony to another. Scripture is a record of a people's determination to hear God truthfully and then to follow God faithfully. The record is in the form of a journey through many centuries. Scripture is the account of the adventure of a journey, not a report on having arrived at a destination. Might I also point out that we ourselves are a mess of inconsistencies, contradictions, and bad ideas? Most of the time it's much easier to see the cultural and historical limitations of the people in the Bible rather than in ourselves. We are still on the journey. It's not a simple song that the Bible wants to teach us to sing. It is a grand symphony that must be heard together with all of its highs and lows, its seemingly dissonant notes that all somehow come together and move in a definite direction.

One reason why DISCIPLE Bible study (created by the United Methodists) is so effective is that it stresses regular reading of Scripture in a way that the Bible becomes the major part of our reading, so that waves of Scripture sweep over us, steeping us in God's way of talking about the world.

Wesley advised that the Bible is to be read "carefully" (using Wesley's *Notes!*). For instance, Jesus, in his nocturnal conversation with Nicodemus, stated that Nicodemus must be born "from above" (John 3:7). There was a time when our Bibles translated the Greek word *anothen* ("above") as "again"—which is not at all what the original Greek means. "Again" was the precise misunderstanding that Nicodemus made with Jesus. Nicodemus wondered how one could be born a second time ("again") when Jesus was speaking about birth that comes from above, birth that comes closer to Wesley's new birth than most contemporary evangelical notions of being born again. In short, we must read carefully if we are to read faithfully.

The Wesleyan Core Term "New Birth" (see *WSB* 1289) is discussed in the context of John 3. The Reformation stressed that we are saved by faith in the work of Jesus Christ in cross and resurrection—the theology of justification. God does for us, on the cross, what we could never do for ourselves—gives us forgiveness of sin, setting right, "justifying" us to God. To this core doctrine of the faith Wesley added that in justification, Christ gives us forgiveness and new life, the new birth. We need not wait to live with Christ in eternity; we are enabled to live with Christ now, here. We are different. It is almost like we have started over and been reborn, now with lives more congruent with what God intended for us. God deals not only with the guilt of our sin but also with the root problem that leads to our sin in the first place. New birth is the beginning of the holy, sanctified life, one of the greatest testimonies to the powerful work of a living God.

"Prayer before and after" acknowledges that we cannot read and understand Scripture on our own. Prayer also puts us in the proper posture for reading Scripture: obedient listening. We pray before in order to place ourselves in the humble mode of listening for a fresh word from God (see *WSB* 692). We pray after (if we are reading like Wesleyans) for God to grace us with the courage and ability to enact Scripture. For Wesley, Scripture is "God breathed." God's word is not really the words that stare back at us, fixed and inert on the page. It's God's word when the Holy Spirit gives life to the words on the page. All understanding of Scripture is grace.

And because we're Wesleyans, we want our reading of Scripture always to be done "fruitfully," by "immediately practising" what we have learned. In a stirring speech of dedication of the grand new Temple (1 Kings 8), we are a bit surprised to find a sidebar on "Forgiveness" (see *WSB* 423). Solomon used the dedication of the Temple not only to praise the wonder and the glory of God but also to ask God to forgive. While the grand Temple was being dedicated, the people in covenant with God were summoned by God for some risky, prone-to-failure sort of work—being God's holy people.

Solomon prayed that we will be forgiven not for misunderstanding God but for disobeying God, for breaking the covenant with God. One reason why there was so much confessing of sin and forgiveness in the early Wesleyan small groups was not that they were obsessed with their sin but that they took so seriously the righteous demands of God. When we go out to practice "practical divinity," to perform in everyday life the demands of God to forgive enemies, to pray for those who abuse us, to give without restraint to the poor, to practice justice and love kindness and walk humbly with God—well, there will be lots of need to forgive us when we fail. Though Wesley didn't specify the sort of prayer we need to pray when we read Scripture, a prayer for forgiveness is fully appropriate just about anytime I read the sacred text. I would rather bend the text to suit my present limitations than to have the text form and transform me into what God intends me to be.

To read Scripture is to read an account of a work in progress. In a sense, the validity and the authority of Scripture are rightly judged by the quality of lives that Scripture is able to produce. Our claim is not so much that Scripture is relevant or useful to our lives (goodness knows, we will enlist almost anything in our efforts to set ourselves up on our terms rather than God's), but that through Scripture, the living God speaks to us and transforms us. Wesleyans believe that Scripture is not ancient history but presently available experience. We believe that because John Wesley believed it and because we have been able to experience it, live it in our lives, and see the force of Scripture within the lives of our own congregations.

In reading the Bible like Wesleyans, we do not ask, "Is this relevant to my life?" Instead we assume the stance of our parents in the faith before us and say, "Speak, LORD, for your servant is listening" (1 Sam. 3:9). The question is the potentially transforming one of, "How might my life be made more relevant to the work that Christ wants to do in the world?" We cannot affirm that Jesus Christ is Lord without obeying him as our Sovereign, without placing ourselves at his disposal, without hearing his word as our summons. Rarely does the Bible cooperate with our search for quick, easy answers or clear, simple ideas of God; Scripture has a way of complicating our notions of God and teaching us to ask even more demanding questions.

Second Timothy states that "all scripture is inspired by God and is useful for teaching, for reproof, for correction, and for training in righteousness," which makes the Bible sound rather close to a rulebook for doctrinal policing. But then the writer adds, "So that everyone . . . may be . . . equipped for every good work" (3:16-17)—a wonderfully Wesleyan statement of the function and goal of our times with the sacred text.

This makes the reading and enactment of Scripture one of the great adventures of life within the scope of Wesleyan Christianity.

CHAPTER FIVE

WE BELIEVE IN SALVATION FOR SINNERS

There is much that we do not know about Jesus Christ. The Gospels record only a few events of his ministry, and nearly all take place in no more than three years of his earthly life. Though obviously talking about the same Jesus, the Gospels differ on some details about him. The facts are few. Yet there is one thing we know for sure about Jesus, that on which all the Gospels agree—Jesus saves. It is as if the Gospels pare away everything from the words and deeds of Jesus that is not directly related to his saving work among us. Jesus saves.

His death is reported in all the Gospels not simply as an instance of the long history of injustice perpetrated by Gentiles against Jews (which his cross surely was) but also as a decisively significant part of the story of God's salvation of the world. And his resurrection is even more than God's defeat of death; his rising from the dead and his return to those who disappointed and betrayed him are a sign of God's vindication of Jesus as the God-given answer to the problem between us and God. Jesus saves. Paul's letters (the earliest of the writing about Jesus in the New Testament) say surprisingly little about the content of Jesus' teaching, still less about the signs and wonders that he performed. Yet all of Paul's letters—in discussing specific problems in early Christian communities, in working out the implications of his ministry—tell the world that Jesus saves.

The Gospels present Jesus Christ as constantly in motion, always on the road. In what direction does he journey? He is always relentlessly moving toward us. Whereas many religious leaders of the day sought to make careful distinctions between the righteous and the unrighteous, the saved and the damned, Jesus got into all manner of trouble (mostly with religious leaders!) for practicing unbounded hospitality. Many of the pious rejected Jesus for his disarming lack of discrimination between the presumed good and the allegedly bad. "This man eats and drinks with sinners and receives them!" was an early and persistent charge against Jesus.

Jesus provoked controversy by inviting himself to the table of sinners and in turn welcoming them to his. In response to criticism that he failed to exercise proper distinctions between the saved and the damned, those within the fold and those without, Jesus told a series of stories

(Luke 15). There was the one about the shepherd who, having lost one sheep, abandoned his ninety-nine sheep safe in the fold and searched until he found the one lost sheep. A woman misplaced a single coin and turned her home upside down until she found it. And when she did, she called to her neighbors, "Rejoice with me! I have found that which I lost!" Then there was a father whose younger son arrogantly demanded his share of the inheritance, ran away to a remote country where he squandered every cent and, when he finally dragged back home in rags, was greeted by the father with the words, "Rejoice with me! My son who was dead is alive again. Let's have a party!"

Jesus told these parables in response to those who grumbled that the boundaries of his Kingdom were too broad, his reach too expansive. So we note yet another truth about Jesus. Not only does Jesus save, but he also saves the wrong people, people nobody thought could be saved, people nobody wanted saved. Jesus was such a relentless, determined Savior that he not only saved insiders, the daughters and sons of Israel who expected to be saved, but also reached beyond the boundaries, saving those outcasts, sinners, and pagan reprobates that insiders didn't really want to be saved.

Paul frequently spoke of this salvation of God as universal, cosmic in scope. Subtly, powerfully, the salvation of God is sweeping over the whole world, catching up everyone and everything in its loving reach. Paul preached a day when

> Subtly, powerfully, the salvation of God is sweeping over the whole world, catching up everyone and everything in its loving reach.

at last God will get what God wants, when at last "every knee should bend, . . . and every tongue should confess that Jesus Christ is Lord" (Phil. 2:10-11). God "desires everyone to be saved," according to 1 Timothy 2:4.

In his own reading of Scripture, in the story of his heartwarming experience, in his observation of God at work in the lives of countless otherwise ordinary people called Methodists, John Wesley was impressed that it is of the nature and work of Christ to save. Wesleyan soteriology (doctrine of salvation) is a grand and glorious thing. So, having spent a few chapters talking mostly about God—Father, Son, and Holy Spirit—we will now talk about the human effects of the God who is. The result of the action of God—Father, Son, and Holy Spirit—upon the world is salvation. Jesus saves.

The God whom Wesley discovered (or perhaps more to the point of the stories in Luke 15, the God who discovered Wesley!) is not only sovereign power and glory but also searching, seeking love (see *WSB* 717). Wesley made a big deal of his own heartwarming experience, the miraculous process whereby he experienced the new birth (see *WSB*

1289, 1522) when his soul was ignited in the transformational service of God. But to tell the truth, Wesley was no great sinner—a more punctilious high churchman, a more highly certified, lifelong child of the church one could never hope to meet. Writing of his heartwarming Aldersgate experience, Wesley expressed such wonder that Christ "had taken away my sins, even mine" because Wesley knew enough of Scripture to know that sometimes God's toughest challenge is to get through to those who think so much about God. Jesus saves by coming out to meet us, by finding us where we are, by refusing to reign in the world without us.

THE SCRIPTURE WAY OF SALVATION

Although Wesley was more a practical pastoral theologian than a builder of theoretical systems of thought, when it came to the experience of salvation, Wesley was at pains to give a systematic, concise, cogent exposition of the subject—his sermon "The Scripture Way of Salvation" (sermon 43). His text for the sermon is "ye are saved through faith" (Eph. 2:8).

Be careful of that word *faith*. In hearing the Letter to the Ephesians say that we are saved "through faith," we modern, pragmatic people are likely to hear this as some sort of call to action, some new technique, a program for our self-betterment (see *WSB* 1493). No. Wesley joined the great Protestant tradition in asserting that we are brought to God

> Salvation denotes our relationship to God in Jesus Christ here, now.

not by our faith in God but by God's faith for us. God gives us faith. In connecting salvation with faith Wesley showed, right at the beginning, that salvation is something that God does in us, not something done by us. Faith is not what we think or feel; faith is what God gives us, a work that God does through us. Our faith is a sign that God has indeed brought us to sure conviction that Jesus saves us, even us.

Wesley opened this sermon by defining his subject. Salvation in Jesus Christ is a present reality. Salvation denotes our relationship to God in Jesus Christ here, now. Railing against those who misshaped the Christian life into a mostly future phenomenon, Wesley said:

> What is *salvation*? The salvation which is here spoken of is not what is frequently understood by that word, the going to heaven, eternal happiness. It is not the soul's going to paradise. . . . It is not a blessing which lies on the other side death. . . . "Ye *are* saved." It is not something at a distance: it is a present thing, a blessing which, through the free mercy of God, ye are now in possession of. Nay, the words may be rendered, and that with equal propriety, "Ye *have been* saved." So that the salvation which is here spoken of might be extended to the entire work of God, from the first dawning of

grace in the soul till it is consummated in glory. (Sermon 43, "The Scripture Way of Salvation," §I.1)

Note Wesley's careful use of tenses. We "are" saved—salvation is a completely present reality. And we "have been" saved—salvation is an accomplished work of God in Christ on our behalf. We need not anxiously wonder about our situation with God. In Jesus Christ, we have been and we are forgiven. We are embraced children of God. We are converted to awareness of our true situation with God, and we are empowered to live a new life in faith. There is definitely a dramatic before-and-after, darkness-to-light, total-makeover quality to Wesleyan views of salvation (see *WSB* 1446). No concept of the Christian life as a slow process of gradual, orderly faith development can do justice to the rather radical before-and-after quality of our being brought to faith. Never one to overly simplify that which by its nature is richly complex, Wesley spoke of three aspects of salvation.

Justification

This is full, gracious deliverance "from the *penalty* of our sins," complete pardon of our guilt against God by virtue of the work of Christ.

> Justification is another word for pardon. It is the forgiveness of all our sins; . . . our acceptance with God . . . all that Christ hath done and suffered for us till "he poured out his soul for the transgressors." The immediate effects of justification are,

the peace of God, a "peace that passeth all understanding," and a "rejoicing in *hope* of the glory of God," "with *joy* unspeakable and full of glory." (Sermon 43, "The Scripture Way of Salvation," §I.3)

In Jesus Christ, in his life, death, and resurrection, God decisively acted in our behalf. God made a way to us, braving our rejection and our bloody betrayal, doing for us that which we could never do for ourselves (see *WSB* 860). Our justification came when God restored the divine-human relationship that we had broken.

Sanctification

This Wesley described as deliverance "from the *plague* of our sinning." Though the church had always stressed God's transformative, cleansing work in us, sanctification became a decidedly Wesleyan emphasis and one of the most controversial aspects of the movement (see *WSB* 994, 1433). Whereas justification is God's decisive work for us, sanctification is God's continuing work in us (see *WSB* 843). By the power of the Holy Spirit, we are graciously given new birth, in which God enables us to begin, fresh and clean, reworked and rejuvenated, having dramatically experienced the grace of God in an undeniable, reassuring, life-changing way. This new birth along with full sanctification are the two great Wesleyan contributions to his inherited Anglican soteriology: "At the same time that we are justified, yea, in that very moment, *sanctification* begins. In that instant we are 'born again,' 'born from above,' 'born of the Spirit.' There is a *real* as well as a *relative* change. We are inwardly renewed by the power of God" (Sermon 43, "The Scripture Way of Salvation," §I.4).

Whereas one might think of justification as the beginning of God's work in us, the precondition for right relationship that only God can fulfill, sanctification is God's daily, habitual, continuing work in us (see *WSB* 940). And, Wesley was bold to assert, sanctification enlists us in the process of our salvation. God works in us to make our cooperation possible. By God's grace, for the first time we find ourselves working with God, rather than against God, enjoying rather than despising the things of God. We become more than passive recipients of God's justifying love; we are active participants in God's love in us and in the world, "working out our own salvation" (see *WSB* 1293) by the grace of God.

American evangelicalism has sometimes characterized the Christian life as a dramatic, instantaneously transforming bolt out of the blue; more typical for us Wesleyans is to view our salvation as a

> **Jesus didn't come to us just to have us think differently, certainly not just to have us feel differently. He came to make us different.**

dramatic but continuing process, begun by God's death-to-birth work for us in Christ, continued in us through our daily walk with Christ and the transformative life-to-even-more-life work of the Holy Spirit. Day by day God continues to work in us by the Spirit. This gradually transformative work Wesley spoke of as "growth in grace." Jesus didn't come to us just to have us think differently, certainly not just to have us feel differently. He came to make us different. And we show the world that he has made us different when we act differently.

In some people, God's salvific, transformative work can be instantaneous, "in the twinkling of an eye," which Wesley judged to be "infinitely desirable." In my pastoral observation, for most of us, our sanctification seems to take time, lots of it. Wesley acknowledged the complex nature of sanctification; God graciously deals with us according to our need and God's providential plan for us:

"But does God work this great work in the soul *gradually* or *instantaneously*?" Perhaps it may be gradually wrought in some. I mean in this sense—they do not advert to the particular moment wherein sin ceases to be. But it is infinitely desirable, were it the will of God, that it should be done instantaneously; that the Lord should destroy sin "by the breath of His mouth" in a moment, in the twinkling of an eye. And so he generally does, a plain fact, . . . whereunto thou art "created anew in Christ Jesus." . . . Christ is ready. And he is all you want. He is waiting for you. He is at the door! Let your inmost soul cry out. (Sermon 43, "The Scripture Way of Salvation," §III.18)

Wesley marveled at the various ways that Christ's power worked in different people:

There is an irreconcilable variability in the operations of the Holy Spirit on [human] souls, more especially as to the manner of justification. Many find him rushing in upon them like a torrent, while they experience "The o'erwhelming power of saving grace." . . . But in others he works in a very different way: "He deigns his influence to infuse; Sweet, refreshing, as the silent dews." It has pleased him to work the latter way in you from the beginning; and it is not improbable he will continue (as he has begun) to work in a gentle and almost insensible manner. Let him take his own way: He is wiser than you; he will do all things well. (Letter to Mary Cooke, October 30, 1785)

Wesley's claims for the power of sanctification's transformation in us are bold:

We feel "the love of God shed abroad in our heart by the Holy Ghost which is given unto us," producing love to all mankind, and more especially to the children of God; expelling the love of the world, the love of pleasure, of ease, of honour, of money; together with pride, anger, self-will, and every other evil temper—in a word, changing the "earthly, sensual, devilish" mind into "the mind which was in Christ Jesus." (Sermon 43, "The Scripture Way of Salvation," §I.4)

We are more and more dead to sin, we are more and more

alive to God. We go on from grace to grace, while we are careful to "abstain from all appearance of evil," and are "zealous of good works," "as we have opportunity doing good to all men"; . . . while we take up our cross and deny ourselves every pleasure that does not lead us to God. (Sermon 43, "The Scripture Way of Salvation," §I.8)

Though orthodox Lutherans and Calvinists, so convinced as they were of the indomitability and persistence of our sin even in our salvation, were highly critical of Wesley's extravagant claims for sanctification, Wesley was so bold as to assert the possibility of "entire sanctification"— gracious divine perfecting of our once sinful natures into the full love of God (see *WSB* 230, 1488, 1501):

It is thus that we wait for entire sanctification, for a full salvation from all our sins, from pride, self-will, anger, unbelief, or, as the Apostle expresses it, "go on to perfection." But what is perfection? The word has various senses: here it means perfect love. It is love excluding sin; love filling the heart, taking up the whole capacity of the soul. (Sermon 43, "The Scripture Way of Salvation," §I.9)

Note the robust, active view of the love of God in Charles Wesley's two great hits, "O For a Thousand Tongues," and "Love Divine, All Loves Excelling." Here is a God who, in love, moves on many fronts against our bondage to sin and death.

> 3. Jesus! the name that charms our fears,
>   That bids our sorrows cease;

'Tis music in the sinner's ears,
'Tis life, and health, and peace.
4. He breaks the power of canceled sin,
He sets the prisoner free. (*UMH*, 57)

1. Love divine, all loves excelling,
Joy of heaven, to earth come down;
Fix in us thy humble dwelling;
All thy faithful mercies crown!
Jesus, thou art all compassion,
Pure, unbounded love thou art;
Visit us with thy salvation;
Enter every trembling heart.
2. Breathe, O breathe thy loving Spirit
Into every troubled breast!
Let us all in thee inherit;
Let us find that second rest.
Take away our bent to sinning;
Alpha and Omega be;
End of faith, as its beginning,
Set our hearts at liberty. (*UMH*, 384)

Glorification

This Wesley characterized as deliverance "from the *presence* of the effects of sin." We are being lifted up by God, lifted out of the muck and mire of our sin, our grubby determination to live without God, and being drawn upward toward the glorious reality that God has in store for us. We are filled with hope as we anticipate that grand, ultimate perfecting that is to be consummated in eternity. Focus on God's promised future gives hope in the present that our ultimate destiny is to be completely, fully united with God (see *WSB* 1508).

The Christian life is more than determined busyness and grim performance of religious duties. It is also mystical unity with the one in whom "we live and move and have our being" (Acts 17:28). Daily we and all creation are being drawn toward God. Daily we are privileged to be among the "first fruits" of God's final transformation of all things, God's drawing of all to himself (John 12:32). Although we are truly sunk in sin, although we are in bondage to death and decay, we are being drawn toward God; we are being reborn, transformed, changed, "from glory into glory, till in heaven we take our place."

In the Wesleys our salvation is much more than some Anselmian (see chapter 2) settling up of divine debts. Salvation is being caught up in the full sweep of God's resourceful, indomitable love:

> 1. Father, whose everlasting love
>   Thy only Son for sinners gave,
>   Whose grace to all did freely move,
>   And sent him down a world to save.
> 4. Jesus hath said, we all shall hope,
>   Preventing grace for all is free:
>   "And I, if I be lifted up,
>   I will draw all men unto me."

8. A world he suffer'd to redeem;
   For all he hath th' atonement made:
   For those that will not come to him
   The ransom of his life was paid. (*HGEL*, 1)

Wesley's deep-felt awe for the active work of God in Christ led him to regard the Calvinist notion of predestination with particular scorn. John Calvin taught what has been called a *double predestination*—a sovereign God foreordains that some will receive damnation, some salvation (see *WSB* 1549). Wesley regarded this doctrine—some are saved in spite of who they are; some are lost in spite of what they will—as not only morally repugnant but also an affront to the grace of God and the death of Christ (see *WSB* 293, 298, 1083).

As noted earlier, Wesley took some pains to reassure his followers that he confessed the full, historic faith of the Church of England in all matters. Yet when it came to predestination, Wesley took the rather radical step of deleting Anglican Article 17: "Of Predestination." Just tossed it. His thoughts were summarized well in a sentence from a sermon on free grace: "The grace or love of God, whence cometh our salvation, is free in all, and free for all" (sermon 110, "Free Grace," §2). God is not simply sovereign, omnipotent, and righteous; God is love (see *WSB* 1515). Though God could have elected to damn all of humanity for our sin, in Christ, God elected all to be invited into a new and loving relationship with God. In Christ, God elected to be our God and elected us as God's people.

Hear Wesley's scathing contempt in a sermon where he said that the doctrine of predestination

> destroys all [God's] attributes at once. It overturns both his jus-
> tice, mercy, and truth. Yea, it represents the most Holy God as
> worse than the devil. . . . But you say you will "prove it by
> Scripture." Hold! What will you prove by Scripture? That God
> is worse than the devil? It cannot be. Whatever that Scripture
> proves, it never can prove this. . . . There are many Scriptures
> the true sense whereof neither you nor I shall know till death
> is swallowed up in victory. But this I know, better it were to say
> it had no sense at all than to say it had such a sense as this. . . .
> No Scripture can mean that God is not love, or that his mercy
> is not over all his works. (Sermon 110, "Free Grace," §§25–26)

Methodist zeal for missions (see *WSB* 1459), Methodist
enthusiasm for organizing and working to alleviate various
forms of human misery all around the world, our heated
evangelistic impulse to reach out, to invite all, to seek and
to save, is surely attributable to the theological notion that
God's salvation is freely offered to all, not because anyone
deserves it, but because God is love poured out upon the
undeserving. All have sinned; all can be reconciled through
the work of Father, Son, and Holy Spirit.

SINNERS

So convinced was Wesley of the power of God to ac-
complish God's desires for us, of the power of God's grace

to work deeply and radically to transform us, that we heirs of Wesley have sometimes been accused of having a too optimistic view of human nature. In Wesleyan thought, the love and grace of God seem to receive more stress than the persistence and power of human sin. But one must not take our stress on God's grace as in any way diminishing our honesty about human perversity. When we commit the sin of not being fully honest about the seriousness of our sin, then salvation degenerates into a trivial matter of basically nice people becoming nicer, good folk getting even better. If this view of humanity were true, then Jesus should have started a self-help seminar rather than gone to the cross.

Surely we have experienced enough human horror in the events of the past century and within the recesses of our own hearts to confess that our sin, our rebellion and alienation from God, is serious (see *WSB* 194, 234, 353, 531, 1122). In bedrooms and boardrooms, on battlefields and sports fields we sin. Nobody could accuse Wesley of having a cheerily, goofily optimistic view of human nature (see *WSB* 674):

> [Our sins], considered with regard to ourselves, are chains of iron and fetters of brass. They are wounds wherewith the world, the flesh, and the devil, have gashed and mangled us all over. They are diseases that drink up our blood and spirits, that bring us down to the chambers of the grave. But considered, . . . with regard to God, they are debts, immense and numberless. (Sermon 26, "Sermon on the Mount, VI," §III.13)

Wesley seems to have accepted Saint Augustine's gloomy assessment of human debilitation and depravity after Eden (see *WSB* 7, 11, 1374, 1377). We have dramatically fallen from whatever God-desired perch we may have previously occupied. We sin. Here is the human situation described in Article 7 of the Confession of Faith: "We believe man is fallen from righteousness and, apart from the grace of our Lord Jesus Christ, is destitute of holiness and inclined to evil. . . . In his own strength, without divine grace, man cannot do good works pleasing and acceptable to God."

And yet God's prevenient grace opens up salvation to all sinners. God is the Judge of all, yet God in Christ shows a determination to make redemption rather than judgment be the final word on us (see *WSB* 1122). In his "Scripture Way of Salvation" sermon, Wesley fully acknowledged our desperate need to repent (*repentance* means "to turn around, to move in a different direction, to be transformed") of our sin (see *WSB* 1143):

> One thing more is implied in this repentance, namely, a conviction of our helplessness, of our utter inability to think one good thought, or to form one good desire; and much more to speak one word aright, or to perform one good action but through his free, almighty grace, first preventing us, and then accompanying us every moment. (Sermon 43, "The Scripture Way of Salvation," §III.8)

Sin is certain, but the grace of God is more certain than our sin. Notice how, immediately after acknowledging our "helplessness" and "inability," Wesley said, "but through his free, almighty grace, first preventing us, and then accompanying us" (see *WSB* 389). Grace, initiating repentance in us and accompanying us through our repentance, becomes God's divine "nevertheless" that enables even us sinners to be drawn into the drama of redemption (see *WSB* 622, 628, 679). Though convinced of our sin, Wesley was even more convinced of God's power to save. We are given new birth that enables us to turn around, to start over, and to have God's image restored in us because Christ dies for us and rises so that he may accompany us to the Kingdom (see *WSB* 14, 1454). Forgiveness of sins, in Wesley, is not only pardon from our sin but also the power not to sin (see *WSB* 423, 428, 1415).

The orthodox Christian belief that we are sinners, all the way down, no matter what we do or don't do, can be tricky to pull off. To believe that we are indeed sinners, prone to rebellion and error, can be an excuse for spiritual sloth. Why try to do better if we are always, no matter what we do, sunk in sin? Why work for the betterment of society if, even after the revolution, the new order is just as fallen and depraved as the old? I think that Wesley would respond that the challenge is to be as honest about the reality of God's transformative grace as we are truthful about our sin. Our sin is serious, but thanks be to God, it is no match for the heartwarming, life-changing love of God.

The transformative power of God, working in us in our redemption, works deep within us (see *WSB* 547). We deeply feel that which Christ has done for us:

> Christian faith is then not only an assent to the whole gospel of Christ, but also . . . a trust in the merits of his life, death, and resurrection. (Sermon 1, "Salvation by Faith," §I.5)
> It is a "sure trust and confidence" which a man hath in God "that by the merits of Christ his sins *are* forgiven, and he reconciled to the favour of God." (Sermon 2, "The Almost Christian," §II.5)

> We [affirm] that inspiration of God's Holy Spirit whereby he fills us with righteousness, peace, and joy, with love to him and to all [people]. And we believe it cannot be, in the nature of things, that a [person] should be filled with this peace and joy and love . . . without perceiving it. . . . This is . . . the main doctrine of the Methodists. (Letter to "John Smith," December 30, 1745, §13)

In our salvation, we are given a new "religion of the heart" (Sermon 33, "Sermon on the Mount XIII," §III.12). We literally experience a change of heart (see *WSB* 72):

> 1. O for a heart to praise my God,
>   A heart from sin set free,
>   A heart that always feels thy blood
>   So freely shed for me.
> 5. Thy nature, gracious Lord, impart;
>   Come quickly from above;

> Write thy new name upon my heart,
> Thy new, best name of Love. (*UMH*, 417)

But Wesley would be quick to add that repentance is neither just feeling sorry for our sins nor feeling glad that our sins are forgiven. Our transformation is of the heart, but it is not limited to the heart (see *WSB* 474, 1501, 1506). We are to bear, in Wesley's words, "fruits meet for repentance" (see *WSB* 1243), works of love that are the consequence of our repentance. True repentance is known through "works of mercy" in which our work for others testifies that God has indeed worked in us. Having been reached by God in love, now knowing that all people are the objects of God's saving love, we reach out in love to all (see *WSB* 1177). The totally consuming, transformative faith that works in the heart and through the hands is what Wesley called "real religion" (see *WSB* 1117). This is why Wesley can't end his sermon on God's salvation of us without stressing our specific response to that salvation:

> **True repentance is known through "works of mercy" in which our work for others testifies that God has indeed worked in us.**

All works of mercy; whether they relate to the bodies or souls of

men; such as feeding the hungry, clothing the naked, enter-
taining the stranger, visiting those that are in prison, or sick,
or variously afflicted; such as the endeavouring to instruct
the ignorant, to awaken the stupid sinner, to quicken the
lukewarm, to confirm the wavering, to comfort the feeble-
minded, to succour the tempted, or contribute in any manner
to the saving of souls from death. This is the repentance, and
these the fruits meet for repentance, which are necessary to
full sanctification. This is the way wherein God hath appointed his children to wait for complete salvation. (Sermon
43, "The Scripture Way of Salvation," §III.10)

I participated in a service of worship where we were
asked to sing a little song that went something like this:
"Jesus died, his blood my debt did pay, taking my sin away,"
a fairly typical substitutionary atonement sentiment. Then
the next verse sang something like, "Now I'm ready joyfully to enter heaven in," or maybe it was, "By his blood I
now can eternity win," or words to that effect.

Can you see why such a song ought not to be sung in
Wesleyan worship? Not only because we've got Charles
Wesley, who could have written better verse in his sleep,
but also because the song expresses a woefully inadequate
and limited soteriology. The notion that Jesus comes, dies,
pays our admission fee, and then checks out is (to our Wesleyan minds) not only a perversion of the biblical story of
God with us but also a denial of our own experience of the
way God's grace accompanies us and prods us along the

way. Our salvation is more than a transaction; it's a lifelong adventure, a relationship, growth in grace.

In our own day, when grand, sweeping, historic Christian views of salvation have sometimes been diminished to little more than "God loves me and my close friends," or else the even more painfully trite, "What about me?" Wesley calls us to reaffirm a more expansive view of God's miraculous saving work among us. God is willing to do so much more within us than simply enable us to "go to heaven when I die" (see *WSB* 892, 1535). And God is busy more broadly even than the work that God is doing in us (see *WSB* 536). Wesley joined Paul and the Revelation to John in claiming that salvation is also restoration (see *WSB* 757). What God in Christ is able to do in the human heart, God is doing for the whole of creation (see *WSB* 228): "All the earth shall then be a more beautiful Paradise than Adam ever saw" (Sermon 64, "The New Creation," §§10, 16).

Charles sang of the love that reigns in heaven coming down to earth: "Love divine, all loves excelling, / Joy of heaven, to earth come down." Our faith is not that we might get the key, the technique, to climb up to heaven but rather that in Jesus Christ, a heavenly God has climbed down to earthly us.

Creation continues. God will not have the rebellion and desecration that currently characterize our life in the world be the last word. God intends to finish what God began in Genesis. Wesley asserted that the whole creation will be delivered from its struggle and travail: "The whole brute creation will then, undoubtedly, be restored, not only to the vigour, strength, and swiftness which they had at their creation, but to a far higher degree" (Sermon 60, "The General Deliverance," §III.3).

Knowing what God intends of the world has consequences for the way that we regard the world. In the same sermon, Wesley said that our wonderment at God's eventual transformation even of the world's animals "may encourage us to imitate him whose mercy is over all his works" (Sermon 60, "The General Deliverance," §III.10). Our belief that Jesus saves all people, even those whom were regarded as beyond the reach of salvation, leads us to regard all people in the light of God's saving intent for all. We try to deal with people as God deals with them. So our belief that God is restoring a defaced creation leads us to be agents of God's restoration to all creatures. Here is the first stirring of a Wesleyan ecological theology.

This world is not some smutty, sorry, decadent place from which we hope one day to be delivered. This world is God's, subject of God's love and providential care. The world shall be restored. Creation shall come to more closely resemble that which God intended in Genesis. And when we work with God, we are privileged to be agents of that restoration, those who offer the world a foretaste of the world's final destiny in God.

Our destiny, we learn in our salvation, is to be swept up in God's great, glorious crescendo of creation and re-creation, redemption and reconciliation, inhabitants of a new, redeemed heaven and earth, witnesses at last to God's grand triumph, at last at home with God:

> Then I saw a new heaven and a new earth; for the first heaven and the first earth had passed away, and the sea was no more. And I saw the holy city, the new Jerusalem, coming down out of heaven from God, prepared as a bride adorned for her husband. And I heard a loud voice from the throne saying,
>
> "See, the home of God is among mortals.
> He will dwell with them as their God;
> they will be his peoples,
> and God himself will be with them;
> he will wipe every tear from their eyes.
> Death will be no more;
> mourning and crying and pain will be no more,
> for the first things have passed away."
>
> And the one who was seated on the throne said, "See, I am making all things new." (Rev. 21:1-5)

CHAPTER SIX

WE BELIEVE IN CHRISTIAN WORK AND WITNESS

Methodists are busy. There is something to be said for the life of quiet contemplation, for the salubrious value of calm meditation on things spiritual, but not much is said about that sort of thing by the heirs of Wesley. Mysticism has not much interest among us. We are industrious. The nascent Methodist movement was the Holy Club on the Oxford campus where the Wesleys gathered other students to practice disciplined living, vibrant fellowship, and performance of good works (see *WSB* 1050). John Wesley churned out scores of books and pamphlets (see *WSB* 483); Charles wrote thousands of hymns. John Wesley logged 225,000 miles, mostly on horseback, and preached some 40,000 sermons, converting an estimated 140,000 in his lifetime. John urged his "traveling preachers" to emulate his busyness, preferably reading the Bible (along with Wesley's *Sermons*!) while bouncing along the roads of England. American Methodists founded hundreds of schools, hospitals, colleges, and universities. Today we are still busy eradicating killer diseases around the world, building new churches, establishing new institutions in Africa, spreading across Asia, busy, very busy for the Kingdom.

I like to think that much of this vitality can be attributed to our theology. An active God evokes active lovers of God. God in Christ not only moves toward us, justifying us, sanctifying us, but also enlists us to join in moving into the world. Of course the Wesleys shared with their Protestant heritage the central conviction that we are saved—justified, sanctified, and glorified—not by our own efforts but by the active grace of God (see *WSB* 1083, 1459). God does for us that which we cannot, in our sin, do for ourselves. In Christ, God makes the first move toward us who could not move toward God and, through the Holy Spirit, keeps working for us, in us, and despite us.

With his Anglican tradition Wesley not only affirmed justification by faith but also believed that true faith is evidenced in and strengthened by our "works" as our response to God's work (stressed in Articles 9–11). Whereas Luther despised the Letter of James, calling it no better than a bundle of straw, Wesley loved James's conjunctive stress on faith *and* good works (see *WSB* 1066, 1097, 1139). Faith is not negated or supplanted by our works; rather, our works testify to the presence of true faith working in us:

Let us plead for faith alone,
Faith which by our works is shown;
God it is who justifies,
Only faith the grace applies.
Active faith that lives within,
Conquers hell and death and sin,
Hallows whom it first made whole,
Forms the Savior in the soul. (*UMH*, 385)

For Wesley, God's grace is powerful, but it is also resistible. God's desire is not primarily to control us but to love us. Therefore, God's love, while working powerfully in us, still leaves room for us to move toward or away from God, though Wesley's primary wonder was for all the ways that God enables ordinary people to do some extraordinary things by grace. Wesley taught that we are responsible. God has created us and enabled us to respond to God's love in our lives here and now. By God's grace, there is a sort of synergy whereby we are enabled by God's grace to work with God. Wesley stressed both the privilege and the obligation to respond to God's overtures to us: "God does not continue to act upon the soul unless the soul re-acts upon God. . . . He first loves us, and manifests himself unto us. . . . He will not continue to breathe into our soul unless our soul breathes toward him again" (Sermon 19, "Great Privilege of Those Born of God," §III.3).

Those of us who are in a justified relationship with God can fracture it through serious neglect of God's appointed means of grace and by our sin. We can backslide (see *WSB* 298), neglecting God's appointed means of grace to the point where we slip away from God. This is covered in the Articles of Religion:

> After we have received the Holy Ghost, we may depart from grace given, and fall into sin, and, by the grace of God, rise again and amend our lives. And therefore they are to be condemned who say they can no more sin as long as they live here; or deny the place of forgiveness to such as truly repent. (¶103, Article 12, *BOD*)

Still, by the grace of God, there always remains for us the possibility of restored relationship. Though we tend to slip up and to slip away, God refuses to allow us to slip out of God's grasp.

MEANS OF GRACE

Our salvation is fully accomplished in Christ, and yet our salvation is also an adventure of growing closer to God, growing more fully into the image of God right here and now in this life. God not only offers us restoration but graciously gives us the means to reach that goal: "By 'means of grace' I understand outward signs, words, or actions ordained of God . . . to be the *ordinary* channels whereby he might convey to men preventing, justifying, or sanctifying grace" (Sermon 16, "The Means of Grace," §II.1).

These means are "ordinary" in the sense that they are ordained by God and in the sense that they are so wonderfully close by us, predictably present for us very ordinary people. Wesley's critics suspected that he was sliding away from Protestant orthodoxy, moving dangerously close to thinking of

> God graciously gives us "means of grace" that constantly feed our desire to do good in return for the good that God is doing among us and strengthen our ability actually to do some good.

works as means to merit God's favor or to certify our smug good standing with God.

Wesley's unvarying stress on the grace of God as the root of everything, including our inclination and ability to do good work, protected him from such charges. God graciously gives us "means of grace" that constantly feed our desire to do good in return for the good that God is doing among us and strengthen our ability actually to do some good. As we await greater perfection of our desires to love God, as we look even for full sanctification, we are not forced to wait idly. We wait in the means of grace, constantly urged on by the practices and ordinary habits of the Christian life.

For instance, Wesley commended fasting as having numerous salubrious effects. He felt that abstinence from food, for a time, helped to clear the way for more intense practice of the presence of God. In fasting, we acknowledge our hunger, and in prayer, we give ourselves the opportunity to go beyond our bodily hungers, now "hungering and thirsting for righteousness" (see *WSB* 580).

As we listen to Wesley, it can seem as if he has an utterly unrealistically high and impossible view of the Christian life. Talk of full sanctification in this life can make it seem as if Wesley has raised the bar too high for any mere mortal to attain. Such a reading comes from too much stress on Wesley's purported end of the Christian life without at least equal stress on the God-given means to attaining that end. Wesley's vision was for the transformation of ordinary women and men into the vibrant, visible saints that God intends through stress on grace as available through character-forming habits and practices of the faith—the ordinary means of grace (see *WSB* 1158). We do not cultivate such practices because we aim to get somewhere with God but because, in God's gracious gift of faith to us, we have already arrived. We're not trying through spiritual practices to attain some unreachable goal with God; rather, we're trying to sustain our relationship with God—through means given by God.

When in the contemporary church this robust theological

affirmation of God's work in us dissipates and we talk mostly anthropology rather than theology—speaking too much of what humanity ought to do and too little of what God has done and is doing—then Wesleyan Christianity begins to sound like a fastidious, rigorous, breathless effort to do good. Good works by us are neither desirable nor possible, taught Wesley, apart from the constantly impinging, encouraging, accompanying work of a living, loving God.

In baptism, the Lord's Supper, Bible reading, fasting, and Christian conferencing, our characters are being formed, not so much by what we do in following these practices but rather by God's use of these practices for us. A primary means of grace is through the imitation of Christ as we become, in life, more like the one whom we, in worship, adore. "It is the best worship or service of God, to imitate him you worship" (Sermon 29, "Sermon on the Mount, IX," §6). Our growing friendship with Christ and the time we spend with Christ draw us closer to Christ. A question that Wesley put to all Christians was, "Do they resemble [the God] they worship?" ("A Farther Appeal to Men of Reason and Religion, part III," §1.2). The disciplines of corporate worship and personal devotion free us from our subservience to the lords of this world so that we might be free for obedience to our true Sovereign (see *WSB* 708).

Even though this book is an exploration of Wesleyan theology, honesty compels me to admit that the great genius of the Wesleyan movement was not so much in its original or systematic theology but in its devising of a web of communal support and private exercises whereby believers were encouraged and equipped to grow in grace. Constancy and habitual, continual practice were persistent themes among the early Methodists. The Christian life was not meant to be left to chance, haphazard meetings with God. We need not sit idly by and wait on God to show up in our lives; God has graciously given us means of grace.

The Lord's Supper was to be celebrated frequently—the Christian life is too demanding to be attempted without regular encounters with the body and blood of Christ. Love feasts were borrowed from the Moravians, putting corporate worship at the center of the movement. Means of corporate accountability were devised, such as small, face-to-face, weekly accountability groups—the Methodist bands and class meetings. The small groups were not only times to share and to pray and grow but also times to hold one another accountable, to be in covenant to work for one another's growth in grace. A host of materials were produced for use in personal devotion. Members were held accountable for performing works of love and mercy as means of grace and growth into Christ, such as making regular visits in prisons (see *WSB* 1199) and providing food and medical care for the poor (see *WSB* 1501).

Although I said that it was not theology but this web of Wesleyan communal and personal practices that was the genius of Methodism, perhaps it is more accurate to say that in Methodism, the practices, habits, and ordinary means of grace were the theology! Theology as more than talk about God, theology as engaged, sustained, disciplined, habitual practice of the presence of God, was perhaps Methodism's great theological gift.

THE SACRAMENTS

Some members of the Protestant family could be accused of lapsing into a neglect of and a woefully unbiblical disregard of the historic sacraments of the church— baptism and the Lord's Supper. We Protestants have at times conducted ourselves as if the preaching of the word is the one and only sacrament. In too many congregations the main event of Sunday worship is not when the congregation gathers at the font or around the table but when the preacher ascends the pulpit. Rather than celebrate the "real presence of Christ" in Holy Communion, as the church has always done, some of our "celebrations" seem to lament Christ's "real absence" from us.

But not Wesley. The Lord's Supper, or Eucharist, played a key role in the Methodist movement and in Wesley's experience of Christian growth in grace. While some Unitarians and Deists in the Church of England had jettisoned the sacraments as sure means of God's grace, adopting a more Enlightenment view of the Lord's Supper as a mere memory exercise that brings to mind the sacrifice of Christ, or baptism as a ritual that mainly signifies something that we think or feel, Wesley affirmed that which his own Anglican tradition had, at its best, always taught: sacraments are specifically, biblically ordained by Christ and are real means of grace.

Wesley added little to the church's orthodox theology of the sacraments; he is mainly notable for what he managed to affirm and preserve of the church's great sacramental tradition in his sacramental theology. (Not all heirs of Wesley have been as successful!) Wesley's own theology of and high regard for the sacraments have rarely been matched by his later-day followers. He preached upon the duty of "constant Communion" (see *WSB* 1325). We are to seize every opportunity to be with the risen Christ. Wesley stressed the *do* in Christ's "Do this in remembrance of me." Communion shows that the Christian life is not solitary but communal, is not passive but active, is not a matter of mere feelings and even words but is an engaging practice.

The Lord's Supper involves a table where we are given fellowship with the Son and with one another *and* an altar in which we are joined to Christ's self-sacrifice for our sin. There, in signs too deep for words, we see the mystery of Christ's work for our salvation. Wesley spent little time trying to figure out *how* Christ was present. He was content to testify to what the church had always taught and what he had frequently experienced—Christ is present, here (see *WSB* 1401).

When it came to baptism, Wesley stressed that baptism

means everything that water means—death, birth, cleansing, refreshment, life, outpouring of Spirit—only now this was water experienced in the name of Christ and in light of the story of our salvation in Christ. In his 1756 "Treatise on Baptism," Wesley asserted Scripture does not limit the mode of baptism. *"Washing, dipping,* or *sprinkling"*—each is an appropriate way for one to become a Christian (see *WSB* 1031). Through something so ordinary, yet so wonderfully mysterious as water, God reaches out to us, saying that which cannot be said through mere water, doing for us that which we cannot do for ourselves.

Citing Acts 2:38-39, Wesley linked baptism to conversion (see *WSB* 1466, 1477). Contemporary evangelical piety often detached conversion from baptism so that baptism became a kind of after-the-fact testimonial that conversion had occurred. But not Wesley. Baptism was a powerful sign that God had claimed us and owned us. Baptism was a promise and reassurance that God would continue to be with us throughout our life's journey as a Christian. In fact, in Wesley there is a sense in which the realities effected by baptism are the basis for later convertings. Our turnings toward God are always returnings to the grace that was promised us in baptism.

Baptism is a washing from sin, sign of God doing something decisive about the problem of our originating sinfulness. Baptism is also sign of our induction into the church, the rite of Christian initiation whereby our membership in the body of Christ is assured. Picking up on Paul's utterly realistic assertions about what God powerfully effects upon the baptized (Rom. 6:3; Col. 2:12), Wesley believed that baptism is the believer's identification with the death/resurrection of Christ. In baptism the old sinful Adam is drowned so that we might rise to newness of life. And in baptism is made manifest the outpouring upon us of the gift of the Holy Spirit (compare Titus 3:5; John 3). God's prevenient grace leads us to the waters of baptism, God's justifying grace shows us in a powerful way our being saved by the work of Christ, and God's sanctifying grace continues to guide us and grow us more closely into Christ.

There is some tension in the Wesleyan theology of baptism. Although Wesley held an orthodox view of the sacrament, he was reluctant to equate his central idea of the new birth with baptism. Conceiving of our growth into grace as a process, Wesley seems to have believed that we are washed, regenerated, forgiven, and adopted in our baptism at infancy. (About the only baptisms Wesley ever saw were of infants—baptism was the English thing to do at birth.) The faith that is evident at our baptism is the faith of the church in the work of Christ; our own faith is incipient, awaiting awakening. And yet on the basis of his reading of Scripture, his experience, and his observations of the work of Christ in others, Wesley felt that as we grow, we fall away from God's gracious offers of baptismal grace. By the time of adolescence, we sin. (Wesley must have had contact with the likes of some of the adolescent boys in my confirmation class!) We are therefore in need of the fresh imparting of the Holy Spirit (see *WSB* 1088), the regenerating, life-changing awakening that is the new birth. The new birth is accomplished by prevenient grace working within us all along life's way. The rite of confirmation, which was unfortunately separated from baptism in the Middle Ages, is perhaps also best thought of as a remembrance of our baptism, a later living out of the promises made to us and the promises made by us (or in our behalf) at baptism. When the new birth occurs, it is for most of us testimonial that God's love was indeed working in us, as God promised in our baptism, bringing us to that point where we could assert the faith that was asserted for us in our infancy.

Note Wesley's changes to Article 17, "Of Baptism," in the Articles of Religion of the Church of England:

> Baptism is not only a sign of profession and mark of difference whereby *Christians* are *distinguished* from others that *are not baptized*; but it is also a sign of regeneration or the new birth. whereby, as by an instrument, they that receive Baptism rightly are grafted into the Church; the promises of the forgiveness of sin, and of our adoption to be the sons of God by the Holy Ghost, are visibly signed and sealed; Faith is confirmed, and Grace increased by virtue of prayer unto God. The Baptism of young children is in any wise to be retained in the Church. as most agreeable with the institution of Christ.

Wesley's study of Scripture and tradition surely made him question the assertion that infant baptism is "agreeable with the institution of Christ." It is a practice that is quite defensible, but not on the grounds of the institution of Christ. Wesley's more extensive deletion seems to have been made on the basis of Wesley's discomfort, after having come to believe in the centrality and efficacy of the new birth, to claim all that the articles seem to claim for the rite of baptism.

Later Wesleyans have sometimes had difficulty keeping these two foci together—sometimes the new birth has eclipsed baptism as *the* decisive saving moment in the Christian life. And sometimes we have lapsed into thinking that baptism was not only the beginning but also the end of our growth in grace with no further growth possible. For most of us the new birth is a kind of postbaptismal turning, a decisive conversion that turns us decisively back on the path that was set for us in our baptism, a sure sign that God is faithful to God's promises. In this sense the new birth becomes that time when we are enabled, in the depths of our being, to "remember your baptism and be thankful."

Of course the church had always defined a sacrament as a means of grace, a gift of God, something that God does rather than what we do. And yet the church has always struggled to maintain the sacraments as also responsive human acts of faith. Baptism is not only water administered in the name of Jesus but also a sign that someone has said,

"Yes, I believe. I will follow Jesus wherever he takes me." So when the infant of Christian parents is baptized, the baptism of a baby (which the church practiced from an early date) is a wonderful sign that God comes to us before we could come to God, a wonderful image of the mystery of prevenient grace. Yet in this baptism the church also asks for response. The parents respond, along with the church, in behalf of the newly baptized and promise to become agents of God's growth in grace in the faith that through our faithfulness and God's faithfulness, this new Christian will surely grow in faith and come to profess and to live this faith.

And the Lord's Supper is a wonderful enactment of the dynamic of discipleship—we come forward to the table with empty hands, showing our need for a gift that only God can give. We are fed. And then we rise and go forth, sent in Christ's name. When Christian worship becomes a passive affair of sitting and watching someone else—the choir and the clergy—speak,

> **The Lord's Supper is a wonderful enactment of the dynamic of discipleship—we come forward to the table with empty hands, showing our need for a gift that only God can give.**

sing, and pray, we haven't done justice to the rhythm of the Christian life. Wesleyan theology has attempted to be conjunctive—we receive the great gift of God's salvation of us *and* we are enabled by the grace of God to respond. We receive the promises of God in our baptism ("I will adopt you," "I will stand by you," "I will equip you for every good work"), *and* we make promises to God ("I will obey you," "I will exercise the gifts of the Holy Spirit that are given to me," "I will accept the new life that is offered me"). In Holy Communion we receive the gift of faith that is beyond mere words, Christ's loving presence made manifest, real, and engaging, *and* we rise and go forth, ready to feed the world as we have been fed, God's gift to the world even as we have been gifted by our time at the table.

FAITH AND GOOD WORKS

While some Protestants made a sharp distinction between Old Testament law and New Testament gospel, Wesley refused to honor this distinction (see *WSB* 1466, 1501). For Wesley, the law of God was a gift of God; the good news of Jesus Christ and the free grace that it offered had definite ethical demands. Faith that is not backed up by visible good works is dead (James 2:26). Good work in the name of Christ is not a substitute for faith in the work of Christ on the cross but rather our grateful, necessary response to that work. Good works are not some devious means of substituting self-salvation for the salvation of God in Christ but are rather our human testimonial to God's miraculous saving work in us. Wesleyans were intent to keep sanctification linked to justification.

Thus *The Wesley Study Bible* discusses *social holiness* (a beloved Wesleyan term) in the context of Leviticus 19 (see *WSB* 146). "You shall love your neighbor as yourself" (Lev. 19:18) was the key verse (see *WSB* 1257). Wesley fully appreciated that in advocating neighbor love, Jesus was affirming the historic faith of Israel. There is no radical discontinuity between the commands of Moses and those of Jesus, the demands of the old covenant written on stone tablets and those of the new covenant written on the heart.

Just as God—Father, Son, and Holy Sprit—is relational, communal, and social, so humans, as the creations of God, are also created for relationship and social responsibility to one another (see *WSB* 237). Thus Wesley famously advised (in his introduction to a hymnal of all places!) that "the gospel of Christ knows of no religion but social; no holiness but social holiness. 'Faith working by love' is the length and breadth and depth and height of Christian perfection" (see *WSB* 146). Christian perfection is perfection in love, love of all, especially love for our neighbors in need whom Christ so deeply loves. The poor, the prisoners, the sick, and the disposed had a special place at the heart of Wesleyan Christianity for essentially theological reasons (see *WSB* 7, 806, 1260, 1347, 1530). When we welcome

> Works for Wesley are a sure sign that the Holy Spirit is working in us.

those who are bereft of resources, we welcome Jesus (Matt. 25:40; see *WSB* 1526). We who had no resources for saving ourselves have been forgiven, loved, saved by the Christ who for our sakes "became poor" (2 Cor. 8:9). Likewise, those who are rich and who have expended so much of their lives in the vain acquisition of wealth are of particular concern because of what Wesleyans believed about the Savior who came to us as one who was poor, lowly, and without home, job, or possessions.

Works for Wesley are the result not of our earnest effort to do good things for the less fortunate, but rather a sure sign that the Holy Spirit is working in us to enable us to do that which we could not do on our own. Wesley loved Galatians 5:22-23, which speaks of the "fruit of the Spirit." Just as we identify a tree by the fruit it bears, so we know that we are in the Spirit by evidentiary fruit of the Spirit—love, joy, peace, patience, kindness, generosity, and all the rest (see *WSB* 1429). Thus Wesley joyfully pointed to the good work being done by "the people called Methodist" as sure evidence that the Holy Spirit had indeed descended in a remarkable way.

Today we are quite right in thinking that the fidelity of a

church is to be judged by more than its adherence to correct doctrine; fidelity is best measured by its fruit. Belief in Christ compels us to act like Christ. Likewise, an individual Christian without fruit, without those qualities of life and gifts that testify to a power greater than that Christian, is rightly judged to be someone who suffers from a paucity of spirit, a failure fully to believe.

Wesley considerably enlarged conventional notions of Christian good works. So concerned was he with the whole person that he read medical books, dispensed medical treatment, and even wrote *The Primitive Physick*, a guide for home remedies (see *WSB* 88). Wesley stressed the need to personally visit and sit with the sick as a sign of God's loving presence. He was convinced that whenever we witness the healing of physical ailments, whether through seemingly supernatural means or through "modern" medicine, we witness a miraculous sign of the restoration of God's intentions for creation, a foretaste of what God wants for all. And when there was healing, it was not merely a personal boon to the individual, but a restoration of a disciple so that someone might resume good works for others (see *WSB* 1211). When someone among us is ill, we don't expect that person to assume any responsibility. All ethical demands are off. Wesley, on the other hand, lamented that person's temporary withdrawal from the campaign of the kingdom of God and prayed for restoration so that the person could resume work for Jesus.

Now if you happen to be saying to yourself, *Fine, but what*

does all this busyness and concern over bodily and material mat-
ters have to do with theology and thinking about God? then you
may have yet to understand the gloriously expansive Wesleyan definition of theology as considerably more interesting than "thinking about God." The religion of the warmed
heart produces religion of the active hands. God's active
love of us produces lovers of God who feel compelled to
act in the name of God. Having experienced the kingdom of
God among us, within us, we want to do all we can to sign,
signal, and witness to that Kingdom in the world.

Fully a fourth of Wesley's sermons focus on the Sermon
on the Mount. Wesley took with great seriousness the Sermon on the Mount as a practical guide to living the Christian life (see *WSB* 1170). That's curious because most of us
today think of Jesus' exhortations in the Sermon on the
Mount—turning the other cheek, not remarrying after
divorce, loving one's enemy—as utterly impossible ideals.
Luther considered that ethically demanding, seemingly
impossible exhortations like those found in the Sermon on
the Mount were there not to tempt us to try to put them
into practice, but to defeat us and thereby drive us into the
arms of a merciful, forgiving God.

In his reading of the Sermon on the Mount, Wesley gave
thanks that Jesus so simply, directly gave us practical guidance for everyday discipleship. He said that the Beatitudes
were a picture of God "drawn by God's own hand"
(Sermon 23, "Sermon on the Mount, III," §IV). (Wesley

described the Sermon on the Mount as "the noblest com-
pendium of religion which is to be found even in the oracles
of God," Journal 16, October 17, 1771). These commands
are not meant to forever frustrate us by their impossibility,
said Wesley, but are meant to be actually practiced with the
help of God. When faced with some seemingly impossible
demand of Christ—such as forgiveness of our enemies—
we are to change the church and ourselves rather than
attempt to scale down the command.

As Wesley encountered resistance to his revival, he issued
an earnest appeal to his critics, attempting to explain
Methodism:

> This is the religion we long to see established in the world, a
> religion of love and joy and peace, having its seat in the heart,
> in the inmost soul, but ever showing itself by its fruits, con-
> tinually springing forth not only in all innocence . . . but like-
> wise in every kind of beneficence, in spreading virtue and
> happiness all around it. ("An Earnest Appeal to Men of Rea-
> son and Religion," §4)

Wesley refused to commend his revival exclusively on the
basis of an experience that it engenders in its adherents.
Neither did he take pride in the birth of a new institution
nor in his movement's conformity to the orthodox faith. He
urged measurement of Methodism "by its fruits," by the
"beneficence" it produces in the spread of "virtue and
happiness all around it." Faith in Jesus engenders good

works for Jesus. United Methodists join Wesley in joyfully linking the mercy of God with the holiness of God, what we believe with what we do, who we are with how we act, praying that our doing will be a public testimony to the fidelity of our believing, and "to spread scriptural holiness over the land" ("Large Minutes").

Martin Luther despised the Letter of James (see *WSB* 1499). James challenged Luther's notion that justification by faith alone (and not works) is the very essence of the gospel. James, thought Luther, came perilously close to ascribing our salvation to our good works rather than exclusively to the work of Christ on the cross.

Are you surprised that Wesley refuted Luther's dismissal of the Letter of James? When this letter was written, said Wesley, "that grand pest of Christianity, a faith without works, was spread far and wide, filling the church with a wisdom from beneath which was 'earthly, sensual, devilish'; and which gave rise not only to rash judging and evil-speaking but to 'envy, strife, confusion, and every evil work'" (Sermon 61, "The Mystery of Iniquity," §19).

In much of the church today, salvation is something that you are to think or you are to feel. In James, salvation is when you talk and walk like Jesus. Though Jesus is mentioned only twice (James

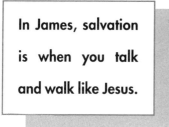

In James, salvation is when you talk and walk like Jesus.

1:1; 2:1), James exemplified the communal, congregational, practical implications of the one who commanded, "Follow me" (see *WSB* 1500). For many of us, worship is that ecstatic, mystical praise and celebration in which we engage in church on Sunday. For James, worship is all that Christians are compelled to do out of love for Christ, in church and out. We are enjoined to be "doers of the word, and not merely hearers who deceive themselves" (James 1:22). Nothing Wesley had to say in scorn of those who accumulate riches and hoard fine things for themselves is as harsh as what is to be found in James: "Come now, you rich people, weep and wail" (5:1).

What is *religion* all about when defined by the life and death of Jesus Christ? "Religion that is pure and undefiled before God, the Father, is this: to care for orphans and widows in their distress, and to keep oneself unstained by the world" (James 1:27).

That's a Wesleyan definition of religion in a nutshell.

CHAPTER SEVEN

WE BELIEVE IN THE
GIFT OF THE CHURCH

John Wesley had his heartwarming, life-changing experience while attending a church meeting at Aldersgate Street in London. As someone who spends a fair amount of time at church meetings, I say that if God could manage to commandeer John Wesley's heart at a church meeting, we really have an amazing God!

Ah, the church. Body of Christ the church may be, but as anybody who has spent much time hanging around the church can testify, it is a crucified body, full of wounds and bleeding. Methodism was a lay renewal movement in the Anglican Church. We never intended to be a freestanding denomination on our own; the goal was the reinvigoration of a rather moribund established church. But that was the way things worked out here in North America—here we became a denomination. John and Charles Wesley lived and died as priests in the Church of England. Though American Methodism became a separate church for all sorts of good and understandable reasons, John Wesley permitted it only with reluctance. He ordained Methodist preachers only when the Church of England bishops resolutely refused to do so (see *WSB* 107). Methodists first named their meeting places *chapels*, so determined were they not to pull people away from their established churches. So Methodism has tended to be a bit ambivalent about our actually turning out to be a church, surprised that God has raised up a movement within the church that has had continuing significance as a church.

THE CHURCH: LOVE MADE MANIFEST

In thinking about the gift of the church we are fortunate to have a sermon by Wesley, "Of the Church" (Sermon 74), to aid us in our reflection upon the gift of the church (see *WSB* 1404). He opened this sermon by saying, "A more ambiguous word than this, the 'church,' is scarce to be found in the English language. It is sometimes taken for a building . . . , sometimes for a congregation or body of people united together in the service of God. It is only in the latter sense that it is taken in the ensuing discourse" (Sermon 74, "Of the Church," §1). Wesley here did not define church as a correctly ordered clergy or boast apostolic continuity, though these were important matters for him. Wesley defined the church as a "body of people united together in the service of God."

We use that word *service* in a twofold sense. The church is where we render service to God through our prayers, praise, preaching, sacraments, and service in God's name in the world. The church is also where God serves

The church is also where God serves us by coming to us, blessing us, speaking to us, giving us the grace to do what God asks us to do.

us by coming to us, blessing us, speaking to us, giving us the grace to do what God asks us to do. Sometimes we think of the worship of the church as something that we do—the words and acts that we offer to God. But worship is also a "means of grace" whereby God does something to and for us. Both of these dimensions are part of the "service of God" (see *WSB* 77, 509). The church is an utterly human institution, with all the flaws of any human gathering. Yet the church is also of God, a rather miraculous creation of God that continues, down through the ages, only because Christ loves the church and has made the church the key to his purposes in the world.

Wesley then noted that the Greek word for "church" in

the New Testament is *ecclesia*, which means literally "called out." The church consists of those who are called out of the world in order to serve the world in the name of Christ. The church is God's answer to what's wrong with the world, but in order to serve the world, the church must be distinctive, different from the world. Wesley next engaged in a rather detailed (and somewhat laborious) study of various texts in which the word *church* appears. (One could never accuse Wesley of putting his theology down on the bottom shelf in an attempt to pander to his audience!) He thus demonstrated that the metaphors for the church in Scripture are rich and diverse, and defy a single correct definition of the mystery of the church. We therefore ought to be hesitant to impose our one, "right" view of the church on a congregation, permitting God and the congregation enough room to define a congregation and its unique God-given mission in order to be faithful.

Wesley highlighted the church not so much as a place of praise and worship but rather as a place where it is clear that Christ "has now dominion over" believers. For these believers, "to obey him, to run the way of his commandments, is their glory and joy. And while they are doing this with a willing mind they, as it were, 'sit in heavenly places with Christ Jesus'" (Sermon 74, "Of the Church," §10). (How typical of Wesley to underscore obedience as a chief mark of the church. See *WSB* 99.) Many of our churches today specialize in having a praise service where the chief activity is praise of God. Much of our worship stresses love of God, heightened affection for God. Along with praise and love, Wesley would surely have us equally stress obedience to God.

Then Wesley indulged in a bit of sarcasm, mocking those whose "faith" is "barely the faith of a heathen; namely, a belief that 'there is a God'" (Sermon 74, "Of the Church," §11). This vague, minimalist religion Wesley dismissed as "barely the faith of a devil." (A fairly harsh judgment upon the "faith" that is currently held by millions of North American Christians, the majority of whom follow no religious disciplines and assemble in no religious gathering but gleefully affirm "there is a God"!) Believing intellectually that there is a God is at some remove from the Wesleyan desire that we obediently follow the God who is there.

At long last (How many of us preachers could get away with preaching sermons as long as Wesley's? Probably more of us if the content of our sermons was as full as Wesley's!), Wesley directly answered his question:

> Here then is a clear unexceptionable answer to that question, What is the church? The catholic or universal church is all the persons in the universe whom God hath so called out of the world . . . to be "one body," united by "one spirit"; having "one faith, one hope, one baptism; one God and Father of all, who is above all, and through all, and in them all." (Sermon 74, "Of the Church," §14)

Wesley said that his definition of the church is both scriptural and in accord with the Nineteenth Article of the Church of England, which says that "the visible Church of Christ is a congregation of faithful men, in which the pure word of God is preached, and the sacraments be duly administered." At the same time he noted that the phrase "faithful men" in the article is, in the original Latin of the articles, better rendered "a congregation of believers," which to Wesley showed that the "compilers meant men endued with 'living faith.' This brings the Article to a still nearer agreement to the account given by the Apostle" (Sermon 74, "Of the Church," §16).

Here we see what was to be a fruitful Wesleyan tension in thinking about the church. Wesleyans tend to hold a conjunctive evangelical *and* catholic view of the church. The church is the worldwide gathering of people that stretches across all cultures and historical epochs *and* the gathering next Sunday in your congregation. The church is that apostolic succession of the saints who have gone before us *and* those who will sit beside you next Sunday who have here and now been summoned by Christ.

Lest we get too mushy in our definition of the church, Wesley stated that the article's definition of the church also qualifies its characterization of the church as the place where "the pure word of God is preached, and the sacraments be duly administered." Not every gathering called *church* meets the apostolic definition. Every church is judged by criteria given in Scripture, standards that are higher than those we often apply (nowhere is warmth, friendliness, or an adorable pastor mentioned in the Wesleyan definition). Dour Wesley pronounced that those congregations "in which the pure Word of God (a strong expression) is not preached are no parts either of the Church of England or the church catholic. As neither are those in which the sacraments are not duly administered" (Sermon 74, "Of the Church," §18). To be the church is to be held accountable to higher criteria than other humanly derived organizations. The church is nothing less than the body of Christ, Jesus' hands and feet, Christ in motion, continuing his movement into the world.

No sooner did the combative Wesley in his sermon "Of the Church" speak of the high calling of the church than the irenic Wesley said that he "dare not exclude from the church catholic all those congregations in which any unscriptural doctrines which cannot be affirmed to be 'the pure Word of God' are sometimes, yea, frequently preached"; even the questionable "Church of Rome" was included in Wesley's expansive definition of *church*: "Whoever they are that have 'one Spirit, one hope, one Lord, one faith, one God and Father of all,' I can easily bear with their holding wrong opinions, yea, and superstitious modes of worship" (Sermon 74, "Of the Church," §19). In the context of the fractious rancor of his day, Wesley's view of other churches is wonderfully magnanimous (see *WSB* 1223, 1385).

Wesley proceeded to what we suspect may be at the heart of what he wanted to say about the church. He quoted Paul that we should "walk worthy of the vocation wherewith we are called" (Eph. 4:1, based on KJV). Wesley settled on the little word *walk*, saying that it covers a great deal: "It includes all our inward and outward motions, all our thoughts, and words, and actions. It takes in not only everything we do, but everything we either speak or think. It is therefore no small thing to walk'" (Sermon 74, "Of the Church," §II.20; see *WSB* 99). The Reformers often defined a church as the place where people sat and heard the word rightly preached and had the sacraments duly administered. Wesley defined the church as a "walk," a place in movement, a journey, not a settled destination. *Church* includes not only our thoughts and feelings but "everything we do." In a world where we tend to compartmentalize our Christianity as something we do in a special place at one special time during the week, Wesley's is an active, all-embracing vision of the church as the body of Christ in perpetual motion.

Then there was a brief digression on our sinfulness in which Wesley admitted that people in church are persons in whom there is sin, noting "our own unworthiness, of the universal depravity of our nature (in which dwelleth no good thing), prone to all evil, averse to all good, insomuch that we are not only sick but dead in trespasses and sins, till God breathes upon the dry bones, and creates life by the fruit of his lips" (Sermon 74, "Of the Church," §II.21).

Wesley really does know church people, doesn't he?

Still, Wesley followed his admission of sin in church with a (typically) Wesleyan affirmation that in spite of our sin, "we are every hour, yea, every moment, endued with power from on high" (Sermon 74, "Of the Church," §II.22). God's grace is experienced in the church as transformation of sinful people into active agents of God's salvation of the world.

Wesley's strong affirmation of the transforming grace of God in members of the church did not deter him from asserting the need for those in the church actually to live transformed lives, to witness, by their lives, to what a gracious God can do. Wesley would have no part in any attempt to describe the church as being "invisible" and "visible." The church is the body of Christ, Christ's visible presence in the world. An "invisible" church is no church at all. Christians are under obligation to make their lives a visible, undeniable testimony to the truth that "in Christ God was reconciling the world to himself" (2 Cor. 5:19). "No common swearer, no sabbath-breaker, no drunkard, no whoremonger, no thief, no liar, none that lives in any outward sin; but none that is under the power of anger or pride, no lover of the world—in a word, none that is dead to God—can be a member of his church," declared Wesley (Sermon 74, "Of the Church," §III.28).

The church is composed of those who are called out of the world in order to work with Christ in saving the world.

Members of the church are under obligation to live lives that are visibly different from the world, that demonstrate to the world the power of Jesus Christ to save sinners.

> In the meantime let all those who are real members of the church see that they walk holy and unblameable in all things. "Ye are the light of the world!" Ye are "a city set upon a hill, and cannot be hid. O let your light shine before men!" Show them your faith by your works. . . . Above all things, let your love abound. . . . By this let all men know whose disciples ye are, because you love one another. (Sermon 74, "Of the Church," §III.30)

THE CHURCH: CHRIST'S PEOPLE IN THE WORLD

Wesley took Luke 17:21 to mean that the kingdom of God is both *within* you and *among* you. The Kingdom in you is that invisible but nevertheless real working of the Holy Spirit within you, and the Kingdom is also among you as God's reign becomes visible to others through the good works that you perform. Thus the world gets to see glimpses of the kingdom of God in the visible good work of those who work out from the church into the world (see *WSB* 1270, 1454).

Church is not just where we hear the word preached or passively receive the sacraments. Church is where we are actively engaged in the love of Christ in the world. Wesley thus ended his sermon "Of the Church" by stressing that the test of the church is in the world, not within the church. Just as God the Father sends Jesus Christ into the world in the power of the Holy Spirit to reconcile the world to himself, so we are sent (Latin *missio*, "to send") into the world (see *WSB* 1459): "As the Father has sent me, so I send you" (John 20:21).

In John's Gospel Jesus said, "I am the light of the world" (9:5). Christ is the world's true light. But in Matthew's Gospel Jesus said, "*You* are the light of the world" (5:14). It takes faith to believe that Jesus is the light of the world. However, perhaps it is more of a marvel that Jesus has enough faith in us to commission us as his appointed lights in the world.

When we affirm the Apostles' Creed on Sunday, we say that we believe in God, "in Jesus Christ his only Son," and "in the Holy Spirit." We believe in the trinitarian God. Immediately after we say what we believe about God, we declare, with equal conviction, that we believe in "the holy catholic church." That's claiming a great deal for the church. Right up there with our belief in the reality of God—Father, Son, and Holy Spirit—is our faith in the reality of the holy, universal church. Sometimes, it's easier for us to have affection for and faith in God than it is to have confidence in the church.

And yet the church is holy because Christ has chosen the church as his appointed means of saving the world. Christ shows up in the church and its worship and service as in nowhere else. Wesley even labeled "Christian conferencing," when we meet and confer with our sisters and brothers in the church, as nothing less than a "means of grace." (Such high regard for church meetings implies, to my mind, that holding boring church meetings is nothing less than a sin!) Jesus has a body. God works through the corporate gatherings of the church to reveal, to empower, and to send into the world (see *WSB* 1425).

A favorite Wesleyan word is *connection*. The body of Christ is noted for its unity, its connectedness. Wesley considered his traveling preachers to be "in connection" with him and with one another. After 1784 and the formal organization of the Methodist movement, *connection* became an indication of conference membership and *full connection* of ordained ministerial status. More commonly *connection* came to refer to all those structures, customs, rules, and values that held Methodists together in a common moment, all those factors that made Wesleyans into a church. Every Methodist congregation is connected to every other congregation for polity, mission, and mutual encouragement and support (see *WSB* 1444). Hymnody surely played such a significant role in early Methodism not only because of the genius of Charles Wesley but also because corporate singing naturally reinforced the emotional, relational, and communal character of Methodism as sacred connection (see *WSB* 1449).

THE CHURCH: GOD'S OBEDIENT PEOPLE

Despite its rather sour beginning, Wesley's sermon "The Causes of the Inefficacy of Christianity" (Sermon 116, which he preached in Dublin, July 2, 1789) is exemplary of Wesley's attitude about the church. The church is full of many means of grace, but it is also the place where Christians receive their assignments in the world and where they are encouraged and strengthened to be obedient to Christ (found at http://wesley.nnu.edu/john_wesley/sermons/116.htm). Interestingly, Wesley didn't expend much time in this sermon thinking about the church. Rather, his focus was on the results of the church, the sort of people produced by the church. Having no interest in speculation about some true, "invisible church" known only to God, Wesley always asserted that the church and individual Christians who are its members have a God-given responsibility to visibly show the world what the grace of God can do. "Why has Christianity done so little good in the world?" is the central rhetorical question that drives this sermon.

In his sermon, when Wesley surveyed the present health of the church in its many forms, he was unimpressed. He didn't devote much of the sermon to doctrine, liturgy, or polity. The thing that really angered Wesley was church people's treatment of the poor. Can the church really be expected to feed and clothe the poor? He held up his contemporary church to the judgment of the ancient church as depicted in the Acts of the Apostles as well as the examples of present-day groups like the Quakers and the Moravians:

> "But is it possible to supply all the poor in our society with the necessaries of life?" It *was* possible once to do this, in a larger society than this. In the first church at Jerusalem "there was not any among them that lacked, but distribution was made to everyone according as he had need." And we have full proof that it may be so still. It is so among the people called Quakers. Yea, and among the Moravians, so called. And why should it not be so with *us*? . . . We are able enough, if we were equally willing to do this. (Sermon 116, "Causes of the Inefficacy of Christianity," §10)

Care for the poor, which the world considers to be an impossible ideal, Wesley treated as a thoroughly attainable reality—if we are willing to make this a priority through self-denial and if we reach out to the help of God's grace. The preacher got down to specific measures that Methodists might take in regard to the poor. Everyone ought to seriously consider leaving all of his or her possessions to the poor, or at least "half your fortune." Knowing that suggestion might be easily dismissed, Wesley pressed his hearers at least to give generously:

> But I will not talk of giving to God, or leaving half your fortune. You might think this to be too high a price for heaven. I will come to lower terms. Are there not a few among you that could give a hundred pounds, perhaps some that could give a thousand, and yet leave your children as much as

would help them to work out their own salvation? With two thousand pounds, and not much less, we could supply the present wants of all our poor, and put them in a way of supplying their own wants for the time to come. Now suppose this could be done, are we clear before God while it is not done? Is not the neglect of it one cause why so many are still sick and weak among you? And that both in soul and in body? That they still grieve the Holy Spirit by preferring the fashions of [the world] to the commands of God? (Sermon 116, "Causes of the Inefficacy of Christianity," §11)

The preacher refused to be put off by our reservations. Wesley didn't leave his preachers unscathed by his demand to give to the poor:

> I many times doubt whether we preachers are not in some measure partakers of their sin. I am in doubt whether it is not a kind of partiality. I doubt whether it is not a great mercy to keep them in our society. May it not hurt their souls by encouraging them to persevere in walking contrary to the Bible? And may it not in some measure intercept the salutary influences of the blessed Spirit upon the whole community? (Sermon 116, "Causes of the Inefficacy of Christianity," §11)

In a style that echoed some of the Letter of James, Wesley mocked those who are content with being mere halfway, almost Christians. If we would be biblical Christians, fine. But let us not overlook Scripture's specific demands that we lovers of God be also lovers of the poor and self-sacrificial livers and givers:

I am distressed. I know not what to do. I see what I might have done once. I might have said peremptorily and expressly: "Here I am: I and my Bible. I will not, I dare not vary from this book, either in great things or small. I have no power to dispense with one jot or tittle of what is contained therein. I am determined to be a Bible Christian, not almost but altogether. Who will meet me on this ground? Join me on this, or not at all." . . .

But to return to the main question. Why has Christianity done so little good, even among us? Among the Methodists? Among them that hear and receive the whole Christian doctrine, and that have Christian discipline added thereto, in the most essential parts of it? Plainly because we have forgot, or at least not duly attended to those solemn words of our Lord, "If any man will come after me, let him deny himself, and take up his cross daily and follow me." (Sermon 116, "Causes of the Inefficacy of Christianity," §§12–13)

It is not enough to say that Wesleyans stress the benign "God is love." Wesley linked love of God to obedience to God. God may love a cheerful giver, but Wesley in his sermon stressed the duty to give. Giving is not optional. Giving need not wait until we feel as if we would like to give or until we find some good, self-serving reason to give. Christians give even as God in Christ has given to us. Wesley dwelled not on Christ's sacrifice on the cross but rather on Christ's command to take up our crosses as well.

Wesley rebuked those "silly outcries of the Antinomians" against the Methodists. (Some critics charged Wesleyans

with being "legalists" with all this stress on Christian behavior and ethics. Wesley called these critics "Antinomians"—that is, anti-law Christians.) He pointed to self-denial
as a central practice of the faith, praising this biblical and
historical testimony on fasting:

> It would be easy to show in how many respects the
> Methodists in general are deplorably wanting in the practice
> of Christian self-denial; from which indeed they have been
> continually frighted by the silly outcries of the antinomians.
> To instance only in one. While we were at Oxford the rule of
> every Methodist was (unless in case of sickness) to fast every
> Wednesday and Friday in the year, in imitation of the prim-
> itive church, for which they had the highest reverence. Now
> this practice of the primitive church is universally allowed.
> "Who does not know," says Epiphanius, an ancient writer,
> "that the fasts of the fourth and sixth days of the week
> (Wednesday and Friday) are observed by the Christians
> throughout the whole world?" So they were by the
> Methodists for several years; by them all, without any ex-
> ception. But afterwards some in London carried this to ex-
> cess, and fasted so as to impair their health. It was not long
> before others made this a pretence for not fasting at all. And
> I fear there are now thousands of Methodists, so called, both
> in England and Ireland, who, following the same bad exam-
> ple, have entirely left off fasting; who are so far from fasting
> twice in the week (as all the stricter Pharisees did) that they
> do not fast twice in the month. Yea, are there not some of you
> who do not fast one day, from the beginning of the year to
> the end? But what excuse can there be for this? I do not say

for those that call themselves members of the Church of England, but for any who profess to believe the Scripture to be the Word of God? Since, according to this, the man that never fasts is no more in the way to heaven than the man that never prays. (Sermon 116, "Causes of the Inefficacy of Christianity," §14)

In a world where there is grave ecological crisis and where the rich get richer and the poor get left out, historic Wesleyan calls to self-denial and simple living may have a new traction among us. Yet Wesley commended practices like fasting and generous giving not because they would make the world a better place, not because they would bring us self-satisfaction or joy, and certainly not because they would be good for the environment. Wesley commended these practices as commanded by Christ and empowered by the grace of God.

Then Wesley charged that the worldly success of many Methodists—due in great part to their abstemious lifestyles—could be the ruin of Methodism:

But why is self-denial in general so little practised at present among the Methodists? Why is so exceeding little of it to be found even in the oldest and largest societies? . . . The Methodists grow more and more self-indulgent, because they grow rich. Although many of them are still deplorably poor ("Tell it not in Gath; publish it not in the streets of Askelon!"), yet many others, in the space of twenty, thirty, or forty years, are twenty, thirty, yea, a hundred times richer than they were when they first entered the society. And it is an observation which admits of few exceptions, that nine in ten of these decreased in grace in the same proportion as they increased in wealth. Indeed, according to the natural tendency of riches, we cannot expect it to be otherwise.

But how astonishing a thing is this! How can we understand it? Does it not seem (and yet this cannot be!) that Christianity, true scriptural Christianity, has a tendency in process of time to undermine and destroy itself? For wherever true Christianity spreads it must cause diligence and frugality, which, in the natural course of things, must beget riches. And riches naturally beget pride, love of the world, and every temper that is destructive of Christianity. Now if there be no way to prevent this, Christianity is consistent with itself, and of consequence, cannot stand, cannot continue long among any people; since, wherever it generally prevails, it saps its own foundation. (Sermon 116, "Causes of the Inefficacy of Christianity," §§16–17)

THE CHURCH:
CHRIST'S BODY IN MOTION

I'll admit that sometimes church can be boring, unexciting. There are Sundays when the Holy Spirit is close and undeniable and Sundays that are blah. I think Wesley would have me add that the church is not supposed to make discipleship thrilling; it's supposed to make it normal. We go to church to practice the faith, to rehearse the faith, to get so good at it that obeying Jesus on Sunday—that joyful obedience—will become the most natural, normal thing we do on Monday through Saturday.

The Letter of Paul to the Colossians opens with one of the most sweeping declarations of the supremacy of Christ as

> the image of the invisible God, the firstborn of all creation: for in him all things in heaven and on earth were created, things visible and invisible, whether thrones or dominions or rulers or powers—all things have been created through him and for him. He himself is before all things, and in him all things hold together. (Col. 1:15-17)

What amazing, wonderful claims for the rule of Christ! Jesus Christ is more than a good friend, a help in time of need; he is the very "image of the invisible God." Furthermore, he was "before all things," the Creator of the world, Creator even of "thrones or dominions or rulers or powers"—everything, the whole blooming, buzzing universe was created "through him and for him."

Has there ever been a more grand acclamation of the glory of Christ? And then the very next verse states, "He is the head of the body, the church" (Col. 1:18). How on earth did the poor old church, with all of its limitations and weaknesses, its sorry record of defeats and disappointments, slip into being Christ's crowning act of creation? His own body? After he created the world, the planets and stars, all beings, all thrones and powers, the great summit of all creation is the church?

This passage from Colossians addresses two contemporary theological errors. The first is the au courant claim, by some biblical scholars, that the divinity of Christ was a later addition to the sweet, simple religion of Jesus by his emotionally overwrought followers sometime after his death. This is a very old theory that, in truth, has no basis. Some of the most sweeping theological claims, some of the highest Christology in Scripture, such as these verses from Colossians, are among the earliest New Testament writings (see *WSB* 1445). Among those who were the first to think about and to follow Jesus, all of them thought of him as the Messiah, the Son of God, the very "image of the invisible God."

A second error is the sentimental, romantic notion that it is possible to love Jesus in a disembodied form—sweet, simple Jesus without his messy body. The church is the grubby, complicated, clanking institution that people added on to the sweet, simple, solitary religion of Jesus. No. Paul's favorite term for the church is *the body of Christ*, as we see here in Colossians. Jesus was no inspired individual speaking to religiously inclined individuals, worried about their individual souls, tending their own personal spiritual gardens. Jesus the Messiah was the head of a messianic movement. His challenge was rarely, "Do you agree with me?" Rather, it was, "Will you join up with me as a member of God's inbreaking kingdom?" The proclamation of Jesus was, from the beginning, a group, corporeal, corporate phenomenon. Something about Jesus brings unlikely people together into community. Something about Jesus demands that we should love him together, in community, as his body.

Thus the faithful reading of Scripture, the doing of truly Christian theology, is a group thing. In fact the Wesleyan in me would go so far as to say that faithful Christian theology outside the church is an impossibility. Christ did not bring us a new philosophy of life, something to think about and calmly consider. He came with a summons, an invitation, a call to take up our cross daily and follow. He invited the whole world not to think about him but to come to a God-given party, a feast for all people thrown by a God who is unwilling to have any left outside.

Perhaps Jesus knew that following him is too difficult and demanding to expect people to do it by themselves. We need help from our friends. Thus Wesley's movement was a group thing, a renewal of the church accomplished by small accountability groups. Wesley's vision of the Christian life was a walk with Jesus, a walk for Jesus, and he knew firsthand that couldn't be done solo. Wesley's

> **Perhaps Jesus knew that following him is too difficult and demanding to expect people to do it by themselves. We need help from our friends.**

goal wasn't simply a better way of talking about Jesus but a better way of being the body of Christ. More specifically, it was the body of Christ in motion. Don't attempt the rigors of Wesleyan Christianity by yourself at home!

So if you have gotten anything out of this book, if along the way you have enjoyed delving into the *WSB*, if you have been edified and strengthened by the insights of fellow Christians, if you have felt the Holy Spirit peculiarly operative in your heart even as you thought you were just thinking about theology, then give thanks to the Wesleys.

By God's grace, the movement of Wesleyan Christianity is still on the move, still gathering those who hear their names called to join in the celebration of Christ's victory and the enactment of the Kingdom, still pushing us out into all the world in Christ's name. Thanks be to God.

INDEX

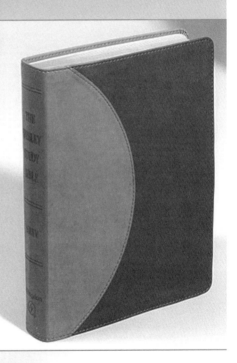